THE MAN OF MODE

by George Etherege

A programme/text with commentary by Simon Trussler

Contents

Swan Theatre Plays published by Methuen London
by arrangement with the Royal Shakespeare Company

The Royal Shakespeare Company (RSC), is the title under which the Royal Shakespeare Theatre, Stratford-upon-Avon, has operated since 1961. Now one of the best-known theatre companies in the world, the RSC builds on a long and distinguished history of theatre in Stratford-upon-Avon.

In essence, the aim of the Company is the same as that expressed in 1905 by Sir Frank Benson, then director of the Stratford theatre: 'to train a company, every member of which would be an essential part of a homogeneous whole, consecrated to the practice of the dramatic arts and especially to the presentation of the plays of Shakespeare'.

The RSC is formed around a core of associate artists – actors, directors, designers and others – with the aim that their different skills should combine, over the years, to produce a distinctive approach to theatre, both classical and modern.

When, just a year after the granting, in 1925, of its Royal Charter, the theatre was almost completely destroyed by fire, a worldwide campaign was launched to build a new one. Productions moved to a local cinema until the new theatre, designed by Elisabeth Scott, was opened by the Prince of Wales on 23 April, 1932. Over the next thirty years, under the influence of directors such as Robert Atkins, Bridges-Adams, Iden Payne, Komisarjevsky, Sir Barry Jackson, Glen Byam Shaw and Anthony Quayle, the Shakespeare Memorial Theatre maintained a worldwide reputation.

In 1960, the newly appointed artistic director, Peter Hall, extended the re-named Royal Shakespeare Company's operations to include a London base at the Aldwych Theatre, and widened the Company's repertoire to include modern as well as classical work. Other innovations of the period which have shaped today's Company were the travelling Theatre-go-round and experimental work which included the Theatre of Cruelty season.

Under Trevor Nunn, who took over as artistic director in 1968, this experimental work in small performance spaces led, in 1974, to the opening of The Other Place, Stratford-upon-Avon. This was a rehearsal space converted into a theatre and in 1977 its London counterpart, The Warehouse, was opened with a policy of presenting new British plays. In the same year the RSC played its first season in Newcastle upon Tyne – now an annual event. In 1978, the year in which Terry Hands joined Trevor Nunn as artistic director, the RSC also fulfilled an ambition to tour towns and villages with little or no access to live professional theatre.

In 1982, the RSC moved its London base to the Barbican Centre in the City of London, opening both the Barbican Theatre and The Pit, a small theatre converted, like The Warehouse and The Other Place, from a rehearsal room.

The 1986 season saw the opening of this new RSC theatre: the Swan. Built within the section of the shell of the original Shakespeare Memorial Theatre which escaped the 1926 fire, the Swan is a Jacobean-style playhouse staging the once hugely popular but now rarely-seen plays of Shakespeare's contemporaries during the period 1570-1750. This new dimension to the Royal Shakespeare Company's work has been made possible by the extremely generous gift of Frederick R. Koch, the RSC's benefactor. In 1987 the RSC, supported by Frank and Woji Gero and Playhouse Productions, and by Eddie Kulukundis, presented a Season at the Mermaid Theatre, London, which included the Swan repertoire and two American plays. In early 1987 Terry Hands became sole Artistic Director and Chief Executive of the Company.

Throughout its history, the RSC has augmented its central operations with national and international tours, films, television programmes, commercial transfers and fringe activities. It has won over 200 national and international awards including most recently the Queen's Award for Export – but despite box office figures which, it is thought, have no equal anywhere in the world, the costs of RSC activities cannot be recouped from ticket sales alone. We rely on assistance from the Arts Council of Great Britain, amounting to about 32% of our costs in any one year, from work in other media and, increasingly, from commercial sponsorship. To find out more about the RSC's activities and to make sure of priority booking for our productions, why not become a member of the Company's Mailing List. Details of how to apply can be found in the theatre foyer.

CAST

Mr Dorimant	**Miles Anderson**
Handy, *his valet*	**John Bott**
Foggy Nan, *an orange-woman*	**Jane Cox**
Mr Medley	**Pip Donaghy**
Shoemaker/Chairman/Footman	**David Acton**
Young Bellair	**Mark Sproston**
Lady Townley, *sister to Old Bellair*	**Joan Blackham**
Emilia	**Jenni George**
Old Bellair	**Joe Melia**
John Trott/Footman	**Edward Rawle-Hicks**
Mrs Loveit's Page/Footman	**David Solomon**
Mrs Loveit, *in love with Dorimant*	**Marie Mullen**
Pert	**Maureen Beattie**
Belinda *in love with Dorimant*	**Katy Behean**
Harriet	**Amanda Root**
Busy	**Claudette Williams**
Lady Woodvil	**Patricia Lawrence**
Sir Fopling Flutter	**Simon Russell Beale**
Smirk, *a Chaplain*/Chairman/Footman	**Timothy Stark**
Sir Fopling Flutter's Page	**Andrew Heron/ Joseph Steele**

Directed by	**Garry Hynes**
Designed by	**Ultz**
Lighting by	**Clive Morris**
Music by	**Ilona Sekacz**
Movement by	**Michael Popper**
Music Director	**Michael Tubbs**
Assistant Director	**Katie Mitchell**
Assistant to Ultz	**James Kronzer**
Stage Manager	**Jondon Gourkan**
Deputy Stage Manager	**Natasha Betteridge**
Assistant Stage Manager	**Kate Sarley**

The performance is approximately 2¾ hours long, including one interval of 20 minutes.

First performance of this production: Swan Theatre, Stratford-upon-Avon, 6 July 1988.

Please do not smoke or use cameras or tape recorders. And please remember that noise such as whispering, coughing, rustling programmes and the bleeping of digital watches can be distracting to performers and also spoils the perfomance for other members of the audience.

Arts Council Funded

Biographies

DAVID ACTON *Shoemaker*
Born: Oxford. **Trained:** Webber Douglas Academy.
Theatre: Seasons at Newbury, Basingstoke, Southampton, York, Bolton, Durham, including Algernon in *The Importance of Being Earnest*, Angel in *Clouds*, Hibbert in *Journey's End*, Charles Lomax in *Major Barbara*, Edgar in *King Lear*, Arcite in *The Two Noble Kinsmen*, Romeo in *Romeo and Juliet*, The Trial (Cherub Company), Moirron in *Molière* (Gate At The Latchmere), St George in *Down by the Greenwood Side* (Donmar Warehouse), *The Oresteia, Serjeant Musgrave's Dance* (NT); UK tours: title role in *Hamlet* (Oxford Playhouse). Tours abroad: Billy in *The Real Thing* (Watermill Theatre), *Tonight at 8.30* (Vienna English Theatre).
RSC: Angelo in *The Comedy of Errors*, Rosencrantz in *Hamlet* (RSC Regional tour 1987). This season: Vizard in *The Constant Couple*, Shoemaker in *The Man of Mode*.

MILES ANDERSON *Dorimant*
Born: Zimbabwe. **Trained:** RADA.
Theatre: Levuska in *Once Upon A Time*, James Joyce in *Travesties*, Antonio in *The Duchess of Malfi*, Norman in *The Norman Conquests*, Schweyk in *Schweyk in the Second World War*, Algernon in *The Importance of Being Earnest*, Turner in *Destiny*, Tattle in *Love for Love*, Aeneas in *Troilus and Cressida*, Captain Plume in *The Recruiting Officer*, Buckle in *Donkey's Years* (Bristol Old Vic), August Strindberg in *Lunatic and Lover*, David in *Before The Party* (Oxford Playhouse and London), Peter Mortensgard in *Rosmersholm*, Philby in *Philby Going Home* (Manchester Royal Exchange), *The Unknown Soldier and His Wife* (London).
RSC: *The Winter's Tale, Othello, Twelfth Night*, Snobby Price in *Major Barbara*, James in *London Assurance*, Hermes Wouldbe in *The Twin Rivals*, Dog in *The Witch of Edmonton*, Sir Frederick Blount in *Money*, Poins in *Henry IV*, title role in *Peter Pan*, Dudley in *The Time of Your Life*, Welbourne in *A New Way To Pay Old Debts*, Mosca in *Volpone*, Sigismund in *Life's A Dream*, Orsino in *Twelfth Night*, Eilif in *Mother Courage*, Antipholus of Ephesus in *The Comedy of Errors*, Lefranc/Claire in *Deathwatch/The Maids*. This season: title role in *Macbeth*, Dorimant in *The Man of Mode*.
Television: *What If It's Raining?, Campaign, Zero Option*.
Film: *Gunbus, Cry Freedom*.
Radio: Numerous appearances.

SIMON RUSSELL BEALE *Sir Fopling Flutter*
Born: Penang, Malaya. **Trained:** Guildhall School of Music and Drama.
Theatre: Theobald Maske in *Die Hose, Points of Departure*, Sandra in *Sandra/Manon, The Death of Elias Sawney* (Traverse Theatre, Edinburgh), Osric in *Hamlet* (Lyceum, Edinburgh). *Look to the Rainbow* (London), The Ward in *Women Beware Women* (Royal Court).
RSC: Young Shepherd in *The Winter's Tale*, Ed Kno'well in *Every Man in His Humour*, Oliver in *The Art of Success*, Fawcett in *The Fair Maid of the West*, Kuligin in *The Storm*, Nick in *Speculators*. This season: Clincher Senior in *The Constant Couple*, Sir Fopling Flutter in *The Man of Mode*, Bob Hedges in *Restoration*.
Television: *A Very Peculiar Practice*.

MAUREEN BEATTIE *Pert*
Born: County Donegal, Eire. **Trained:** Royal Scottish Academy of Music and Drama.
Theatre: Seasons at Dundee, Perth, Edinburgh, Coventry, Manchester, Glasgow, including title role in *Major Barbara*, Miss Giddons in *The Innocents*, Rosalind in *As You Like It*, Pegeen Mike in *Playboy of the Western World*, Lady Macbeth in *Macbeth*, Portia in *The Merchant of Venice*, Isabella in *Edward II*. Emilia in *Othello* (Lyric Hammersmith), Headmistress in *Daisy Pulls It Off* (Globe). Scottish tour as Titania in *A Midsummer Night's Dream*. Tour to Lanzarote and Edinburgh Festival '87 in *Marie of Scotland* with own theatre company.

RSC: Tour abroad in *The Hollow Crown*. This season: Lady Lurewell in *The Constant Couple*, Lady Macduff in *Macbeth*, Pert in *The Man of Mode*.
Television: *Truckers, Troubles and Strife, The Campbells*.
Radio: *Can You Hear Me?* (awarded the Pye Radio Best Actress award 1981).
Other: Formed own theatre company with partner Judy Sweeney called Swaive Kinooziers.

KATY BEHEAN *Belinda*
Trained: National Youth Theatre and RADA.
Theatre: includes Olivia in *Night Must Fall* (Greenwich), Emilia in *Othello* (London Theatre of Imagination).
RSC: Solveig in *Peer Gynt*, Wendy in *Peter Pan*, Marianne in *Tartuffe*. This season: Belinda in *The Man of Mode*, Philomele in *The Love of the Nightingale*.
Television: includes *Sophia and Constance, Chekhov in Yalta, The Lenny Henry Show, Insurance Man, Molière*.
Film: includes *Hidden City, Wetherby, Comrades, Tai Pan*.

JOAN BLACKHAM *Lady Townley*
Born: Wolverhampton. **Trained:** New College of Speech and Drama, London.
Theatre: Seasons at Crewe, Cheltenham, Harrogate, Leeds and Derby, including Ann in *Slag*, Robin Hood in *Babes in the Wood*, Sarah in *The Norman Conquests*, Susan in *Abigail's Party*, Jennifer in *Masterpieces*, Marion in *Absurd Person Singular*, Marion in *Mr Director* (Orange Tree), Fay in *Loot* (Lyric Studio, Hammersmith & Arts Theatre), Edna Klein in *Children of a Lesser God* (Mermaid and Albery Theatres), Virginia Woolf in *The Voyage Home* (Tabard & King's Head), UK tours of *Under Milk Wood*, Sister in *Whose Life Is It Anyway?*, Julia in *The Ghost Train*, Laura in *Multiple Choice*.
RSC: This season: Margaret in *Across Oka*, Lady Townley in *The Man of Mode*, Chorus/Queen in *The Love of the Nightingale*, Education Project – Goneril in *King Lear*.
Television: *To The Manor Born, Take a Letter Mr Jones, Sweet Sixteen, Angels, Bird of Prey 2, Brookside, Chocky's Challenge, A Small Problem, Boon, Paradise Postponed, Intimate Contact, Home to Roost, Hannay*.
Film: *Return to Waterloo, Plenty, The Zip*.

JOHN BOTT *Handy*
Born: Douglas, Isle of Man.
Theatre: Seasons at Northampton and Worcester. Pradah Singh in *Conduct Unbecoming* (Queens), Duke of Venice in *Othello* (Mermaid), Reverend Cotton in *Cato Street* (Young Vic), Bishop of Assisi in *Francis* (Greenwich), Ernest in *Bedroom Farce*, Hirst in *No Man's Land*, Pop in *The Pyjama Game* (UK tours), *Sherlock Holmes, Travesties* (USA), *Relative Values* (Vienna), *Look Back In Anger, A Man For All Seasons* (Hong Kong). One-man show *Man from Mann* (New End Theatre).
RSC: Titus Lartius in *Coriolanus*, Soothsayer in *Julius Caesar*, Soothsayer in *Antony and Cleopatra*, Count Von Stalberg in *Sherlock Holmes*, Bennett in *Travesties*, Banks in *Wild Oats*, Balthazar in *The Comedy of Errors*. This season: Old Man/Old Siward in *Macbeth*, Handy in *The Man of Mode*, Gaoler in *Restoration*.
Television: *Anna of the Five Towns, Cover Her Face, The Charmer*.
Radio: Ex-member of BBC Radio Drama Company. *The Archers, Man from Mann*.
Writing: *The Figure of the House, See The Players Well Bestow'd, The Script*.

JANE COX *Foggy Nan*
Born: London. **Trained:** Rose Bruford College.
Theatre: Seasons at Contact Theatre, Manchester, Forum Theatre Wythenshawe, Coliseum Oldham, Octagon Theatre, Bolton, including Mrs Roberts in *Scraps*, Violet in *Steaming*, Rachael in *Season's Greetings*, Mrs Smilgin/Landlady in *The Mother*, Reeny in *Breezeblock Park*, Liz Piper in *All in Good Time*, Mrs Peachum/Mrs Trapes in *The Beggar's Opera*. For Belt and

Braces Company: Rosie Laird in *Coming Up* (Half Moon and UK tour). For Monstrous Regiment Company: Darya in *The Execution* (ICA and UK tour) and Quiet Kate in *Calamity* (Tricycle, UK tour and International Women's Theatre Festival, Rome).
RSC: This season: Tessa in *Across Oka*, Foggy Nan in *The Man of Mode*, Mrs Wilson in *Restoration*.
Television: *The Monocled Mutineer, Bulman, Return of the Antelope.*
Radio: *Gearchange.*
Other: Musical Director & Composer for *Calamity, Handsome Terms* (Coventry), *Where the Fenians Sleep* (Pitprop), *Chalking the Flags* (Theatre-Mobile). Founder member of Bruvvers Theatre, Newcastle. Also TIE work at Leeds, Coventry, Sheffield and Others.

PIP DONAGHY *Medley*
Born: North Yorkshire. **Trained:** London Drama Centre.
Theatre: Seasons at Sheffield, Nottingham, Cambridge and Liverpool. Jesus Christ in *The Passion*, Clytemnestra in *The Oresteia*, Sir Lucius O Trigger in *The Rivals*, Napoleon in *Animal Farm*, *The Wandering Jew*, *Countrymania* (NT). UK Tours: *Waiting for Godot* (with Not the National Theatre), *The Speakers, Fanshen, Devil's Island, Say Your Prayers* (with Joint Stock), *Bitter Apples, Trees in the Wind, The Garden of England* (with 7:84). Tours abroad: *The Oresteia* (Epidaurus).
RSC: Sir Harry Wildair in *The Constant Couple*, Medley in *The Man of Mode*, Tereus in *The Love of the Nightingale*.
Television: *Invisible Man, Pickwick Papers, Oliver Twist, Alice in Wonderland.*
Film: *1984.*

JENNI GEORGE *Emilia*
Born: London. **Trained:** Central School of Speech and Drama.
Theatre: Seasons at Leeds, Manchester and Ipswich, including *A Midsummer Night's Dream*, Biddy in *Great Expectations*, Tweeny in *The Admirable Crichton*, Cymbeline, Maria in *Twelfth Night*, Adriana in *The Comedy of Errors*, Josephine Baker in *Piaf*, Alea in *Split Second* (Lyric, Hammersmith). UK Tour of *Getting Plenty* (Temba Theatre Group).
RSC: Second Queen in *The Two Noble Kinsmen*, Callis in *The Rover*, Queen Tota in *The Fair Maid of the West*, Anna in *Dido and Aeneas, Peacemaker* (RSC Festival). This season: Parly in *The Constant Couple*, Emilia in *The Man of Mode*, Niobe in *The Love of the Nightingale*.
Television: *Jury, Just Good Friends, Johnny Jarvis, Frontline, In Sickness and In Health.*

GARRY HYNES *Director*
Theatre: In 1975 formed the Druid Theatre Company in Galway, for whom she has directed *Playboy of the Western World, Wood of the Whispering, Conversations on a Homecoming, Bailegangaire, 'Tis Pity She's a Whore, A Touch of the Poet, Factory Girls*. Directed *A Whistle in the Dark* (Abbey Theatre, Dublin). She has twice won the Harveys award for Director of the Year in 1983 and 1985 and was nominated for a SWET award in 1985. She received an Honorary Doctorate in 1987 from the National Council for Education Award in Ireland.
RSC: This season: *The Man of Mode, The Love of the Nightingale.*

PATRICIA LAWRENCE *Lady Woodvil*
Trained: Royal Academy of Dramatic Art.
Theatre: Seasons at Leatherhead, Salisbury, Coventry and Greenwich, including Emilia in *Othello*, Helene Hanff in *84 Charing Cross Road*, Ethel in *On Golden Pond*, Mrs Petkoff in *Arms and the Man*, *West of Suez* (Royal Court and Cambridge Theatre), *Funny Sunday, Sometime Never* (Fortune), *Dead Ringer* (Duke of Yorks), *Heat of the Day* (Donmar Warehouse), *Naked* (Old Red Lion). UK tours of *Five Finger Exercise, Dead Ringer, Heat of the Day*.
RSC: This season: Eileen in *Across Oka*, Lady Woodvil in *The Man of Mode*,

Old Lady Are in *Restoration*.
Television: includes *Intimate Strangers, Anna Karenina, Telford's Change, Barriers, To Serve Them All My Days, Tenko, Vanity Fair, A Very Peculiar Practice, Brimstone and Treacle, Son of Man*, and many other single plays.
Film: *The Hireling, The Millionairess, O Lucky Man, A Room with a View.*

JOE MELIA *Old Bellair*
Theatre: *One to Another, Irma La Douce, Beyond The Fringe, Happy End, A Day in the Death of Joe Egg, Trixie and Baba, Who's Who of Flapland, Leonardo's Last Supper, Noonday Demons, Enter Solly Gold, Rabelais, The Sandboy, The Threepenny Opera, Who's Who, Aladdin, Birds of Passage, Number One* (London).
RSC: Ubell Untermeyer in *Section 9*, Froylan in *The Bewitched*, Bill in *The Can-Opener*, Sgt Fielding in *Too True to be Good*, John Dory in *Wild Oats*, Len Bonny in *Privates on Parade*, Touchstone in *As You Like It*, Second Murderer in *Richard III*, Thersites in *Troilus and Cressida*, *The Swan Down Gloves*, Maurice in *Good*, Isaac Levine in *Flight*, Autolycus in *The Winter's Tale*, Sir Robert Walpole in *The Art of Success*, Mayor/Mullisheg, King of Fez in *The Fair Maid of the West*, Chief of Police in *The Balcony*. This season: Alderman Smuggler in *The Constant Couple*, Old Bellair in *The Man of Mode*.

KATIE MITCHELL *Assistant Director*
Theatre: Started working in theatre as a Production Assistant at the King's Head Theatre. Assistant Director for Paines Plough, The Writer's Company. Also Assistant Director on *Joking Apart* (Belgrade Theatre, Coventry). Directed *Gobstopper* and *Hatikva* (King's Head).
RSC: This season: Assistant Director for *Much Ado About Nothing, The Plain Dealer, The Man of Mode, Education Project – King Lear.*

MARIE MULLEN *Mrs Loveit*
Born: Sligo, Ireland.
Theatre: Founder member of Druid Theatre Company Galway in 1975 for whom work includes Widow Quinn in *Playboy of the Western World*, Amanda in *The Glass Menagerie*, Mary in *Bailegangaire*, Nora in *A Doll's House*, Beatrice in *Much Ado About Nothing*, Nora in *Touch of the Poet*, Rebecca in *Factory Girls*. **RSC:** This season: Mrs Loveit in *The Man of Mode*, Procne in *The Love of the Nightingale*.

MICHAEL POPPER *Movement*
Has performed with Ballet Rambert, Direct Current and 2nd Stride on television, in film, and as a soloist, appearing last year with Women's Comedy Workshop, in Pete Brook's production *The Sleep*, and with the Gateway to Freedom Tango Co-operative. He has choreographed for theatre, television and video including *A Personal Appearance*, and *Mary, Mary* for Direct Current, and *Narcissus Finds His Soul* for Gateway to Freedom. Earlier this year he directed Heartbroke for the vocal-theatre group Vocem, and played Gudgeon in *Le Vallon* by Simone Benmussa for the Compagnie Renaud-Barrault.
RSC: This season: *The Man of Mode.*

EDWARD RAWLE-HICKS *John Trott/Footman*
Born: London.
Theatre: Wharton in *Another Country* (Queens Theatre), Daniel in *That Summer* (Hampstead).
RSC: Sasha in *Breaking the Silence* (Pit and Mermaid). This season: Matty in *Across Oka*, John Trott/Footman in *The Man of Mode*, Actor Playing Hippolytus/Male Chorus/Sailor in *The Love of the Nightingale*, Education Project – King of France/Oswald in *King Lear*.
Television: *Penmaric, To Serve them All My Days, Play for Today – Country, Changing Partners, Missing From Home, Summer Lightning, By the Sword Divided, Paradise Postponed, Long Live the King, Casualty, Bulman, East of Ipswich, Tumbledown.*

AMANDA ROOT *Harriet*

Born: Chelmsford, Essex. **Trained:** Webber Douglas Academy.
Theatre: Essie in *The Devil's Disciple* (Leeds Playhouse). *The Dragon's Tail* (Apollo), Adela in *The House of Bernarda Alba* (Globe).
RSC: Hermia in *A Midsummer Night's Dream*, Juliet in *Romeo and Juliet* (1983 RSC/NatWest Regional Tour and Stratford), Jessica in *The Merchant of Venice*, Moth in *Love's Labour's Lost*, Lucy in *Today*. This season: Angelica in *The Constant Couple*, Lady Macbeth in *Macbeth*, Harriet in *The Man of Mode*. RSC Festivals: Not The RSC Festival 1984/85: Neuroza in *Tell Me Honestly* (Stratford, Newcastle and London).
Television: *This Lightning Always Strikes Twice*, *Ladies In Charge*, *The South Bank Show – Gothic*, *Jackanory*, *Mary Rose*.
Film: Voice-over for animated cartoon *The Big Friendly Giant* by Roald Dahl (to be released Dec. 1988).
Other: Recently directed and produced children's pantomime for London hospitals.

ILONA SEKACZ *Composer*

Theatre: Includes: *A Handful of Dust*, *La Ronde* (Shared Experience), *A Patriot For Me* (Haymarket), *Major Barbara*, *Saint Joan*, *The Real Inspector Hound* and *The Critic*, *The Cherry Orchard* (NT), *The Glass Menagerie* (Greenwich), *Countrymania*, *Cat on a Hot Tin Roof* (NT).
RSC: *King Lear*, *Twelfth Night*, *Henry VIII*, *Measure for Measure*, *The Merchant of Venice*, Bond's *Lear*, *Golden Girls*, *Troilus and Cressida*, *Les Liaisons Dangereuses* (London & Broadway), *Mephisto*, *The Danton Affair*, *Cymbeline*, *The Jew of Malta*, *Indigo*, *A Question of Geography*. This season: *Across Oka*, *The Man of Mode*.
Television: Includes *Boys From the Blackstuff*, *Queen of Hearts*, *Freud*, *Dutch Girls*, *Bluebell*, *The Insurance Man*, *Unnatural Causes*, *Northanger Abbey*, *Love Match*, *Hedgehog Wedding*, *Rat in the Skull*, *The Importance of Being Earnest*, *Intimate Contact*, *Imaginary Friends*, *Dead Lucky*, *The Index Has Gone Fishing*, *The Final Run*, *Run for the Lifeboat*, *The Picnic*, *Hunting the Squirrel*.
Radio: Includes *Romeo and Juliet*, *Cymbeline*, *Macbeth*, *Richard II*, *Oedipus*, *Dreamplay*, *Tom Jones*, *Kipps*.

DAVID SOLOMON *Mrs Loveit's Page/Footman*

Born: Madras, India. **Trained:** R.A.D.A.
RSC: This season: Footman in *The Constant Couple*, Seyton in *Macbeth*, Mrs Loveit's Page/Footman in *The Man of Mode*.

MARK SPROSTON *Young Bellair*

Theatre: Seasons at Contact Theatre Manchester, Haymarket Theatre Leicester, Palace Theatre Westcliff including Henry IV in *Henry IV Part I*, Barry in *Saved*, Townley in *London Cuckolds*, *The Devil and the Good Lord* (Lyric, Hammersmith), Jean in *Journeys Among the Dead* (Riverside Studios), *The Three Sisters* (Shared Experience and UK tour), Enobarbus in *Antony and Cleopatra* (UK tour).
RSC: Mario in *They Shoot Horses Don't They?* Abraham in *Romeo and Juliet*, Pressman 2 in *The Great White Hope*. This season: Clincher Junior in *The Constant Couple*, Angus/First Murderer in *Macbeth*, Young Bellair in *The Man of Mode*.
Television: *Wrinkly*. **Film:** *Sammy and Rosie Get Laid*, *A Hazard of Hearts*.

TIMOTHY STARK *Smirk*

Trained: Corona Stage School. **Theatre:** *Antigone* (NT).
RSC: This season: Nikolai in *Across Oka*, Smirk in *The Man of Mode*, Messenger in *Restoration*.
Television: *The Professionals*, *Sergeant Cribb*, *Doctor's Daughters*, *Treasure Seekers*, *Bergerac*, *No Place Like Home*, *Vice Versa*, *Number 10*, *Little Eyolf*, *Children's Island*, *The Drummonds*, *William Tell*.
Film: *Shocking Accident* (Oscar for Best Short Film).
Radio: *The Years Between*, *A Great Day for Bonzo*, *The Haunted Abbey*.

MICHAEL TUBBS *Music Director*

Education: Cambridge University, Guildhall School of Music.
Theatre: After five years working in repertory theatres, joined RSC as Deputy Music Director in 1967. Music Director for most productions at the RST and several at The Other Place and Swan Theatre since then. Arranged the music for *Twelfth Night*, *Piaf*, *The Suicide*. Wrote music for TOP's first production – Buzz Goodbody's *King Lear*.

ULTZ *Designer*

Theatre: Designs in Repertory: seasons at Glasgow Citizens', Birmingham Rep, Stratford East, Exeter. Designs for John Caird's production of *As You Like It* (Klarateatern, Stockholm), Adrian Noble's production of *Twelfth Night* (Ginza Saison Theatre, Tokyo), *The Cherry Orchard* (Stratford, Ontario). As writer/director/designer in collaboration with Martin Duncan: *The Amusing Spectacle of Cinderella*, *A Night in Old Peking* (Lyric, Hammersmith), *Merrie Pranckes* (ICA). *All in All, Leonore!* (Sheffield Crucible) and a new adaptation of Goldoni's *The Servant of Two Masters* (Cambridge Theatre Company). As director/designer: *A Midsummer Night's Dream* at the National Arts Centre Ottawa; *Pericles*, *The Taming of the Shrew* (Stratford East). *Perikles* (Stockholms Stadsteater).
Designs for the RSC: *Good* (London and Broadway), *The Twin Rivals*, *Naked Robots*, *Our Friends in the North*, *The Comedy of Errors*, *The Merchant of Venice*, *The Art of Success*. Designer and co-director for *Deathwatch/The Maids*. This season: *The Constant Couple*, *The Man of Mode*.

CLAUDETTE WILLIAMS *Busy*

Born: Jamaica. **Trained:** Guildhall School of Music and Drama.
Theatre: *Spell No. 7* (Donmar Warehouse), Odessa in *Amen Corner*, Chorus in *Medea* (Young Vic and Theatr Clwyd). *Ending*, *The Four Seasons* (Edinburgh Festival). UK Tours: *Jelly Roll Soul* (Grand Union Theatre Group).
RSC: This season: Tom Errand's Wife in *The Constant Couple*, Busy in *The Man of Mode*, Chorus in *The Love of the Nightingale*.
Television: *Rainbow*, *To Have and To Hold*, *Fighting Back*, *Happy Families*, *Adrian Mole*, *The Cage*.

UNDERSTUDIES

David Acton *Sir Fopling Flutter*
Maureen Beattie *Mrs Loveit*
Joan Blackham *Lady Woodvil*
John Bott *Old Bellair*
Jane Cox *Belinda/Lady Townley/Busy*
Edward Rawle-Hicks *Young Bellair*
David Solomon *Dorimant*
Mark Sproston *Medley*
Timothy Stark *Handy/Shoemaker*
Claudette Williams *Pert/Harriet/Emilia/Foggy Nan*

Royal Shakespeare Company

Sponsored by

Royal Insurance

RSC REPERTOIRE 1988

Stratford-upon-Avon Box Office (0789) 295623

ROYAL SHAKESPEARE THEATRE

Much Ado About Nothing
by William Shakespeare

Macbeth
by William Shakespeare

The Tempest
by William Shakespeare

The Plantagenets
adapted from William Shakespeare's
Henry VI, Parts I, II, III and Richard III

Henry VI, The Rise of **Edward IV**

Richard III His Death

SWAN THEATRE

The Constant Couple
by George Farquhar

The Plain Dealer
by William Wycherley

The Man of Mode
by George Etherege

Restoration
by Edward Bond

THE OTHER PLACE

Across Oka
by Robert Holman

King John
by William Shakespeare
Supported by *Hancox garden machinery*

The Love of the Nightingale
by Timberlake Wertenbaker

Campesinos
by Nick Darke

London Box Office (01) 638 8891

BARBICAN THEATRE

Twelfth Night
by William Shakespeare

The Merchant of Venice
by William Shakespeare

Julius Caesar
by William Shakespeare

Three Sisters
by Anton Chekhov

The Taming of the Shrew
by William Shakespeare
Supported by
Ladbroke Group plc

Measure for Measure
by William Shakespeare

THE PIT

Cymbeline
by William Shakespeare

Fashion
by Doug Lucie

Temptation
by Vaclav Havel

The Revenger's Tragedy
by Cyril Tourneur

Titus Andronicus
by William Shakespeare

Hyde Park
by James Shirley

The Bite of the Night
by Howard Barker

Divine Gossip
by Stephen Lowe

RSC/ALMEIDA SEASON

Box Office (01) 359 4404/226 4488
2 August – 1 October 1988

Hello and Goodbye
by Athol Fugard

Keeping Tom Nice
by Lucy Gannon

Oedipus
by Seneca
adapted by Ted Hughes

RSC in the West End

PALACE THEATRE

Box Office (01) 437 6834
Les Misérables
The Victor Hugo Musical

AMBASSADORS THEATRE

Box Office (01) 836 6111
Les Liaisons Dangereuses
by Christopher Hampton

SAVOY THEATRE until 6 August

Box Office (01) 836 8888
Kiss Me Kate
by Cole Porter

Royal Shakespeare Company
Incorporated under Royal Charter as the
Royal Shakespeare Theatre
Patron Her Majesty the Queen
President Sir Kenneth Cork
Chairman of the Council Geoffrey A Cass
Vice Chairman Dennis L Flower
Advisory Direction Peggy Ashcroft, Peter Brook, Trevor Nunn
Artistic Director and Chief Executive Terry Hands
Direction Bill Alexander, John Barton, John Caird,
Ron Daniels, Terry Hands, Barry Kyle, Adrian Noble
Director Emeritus Trevor Nunn
Director 1988 Stratford-upon-Avon Season Adrian Noble
Director 1988 London Season Bill Alexander

Administration
John Bradley *Technical Services Administrator*
David Brierley *General Manager*
Peter Harlock *Publicity Controller*
James Langley *Production Controller*
Tim Leggatt *Planning Controller*
Genista McIntosh *Senior Administrator*
James Sargant *Barbican Administrator*
William Wilkinson *Financial Controller*

Deputies
Stephen Browning *Publicity (London)*
David Fletcher *Finance*
Gillian Ingham *Publicity (Stratford)*
Carol Malcolmson *Planning*

Heads of Department
Cicely Berry *Voice*
Siobhan Bracke *Casting*
Colin Chambers *Literary*
Andy Clark *Data Processing*
Brian Davenhill *Scenic Workshops*
Tony Hill *Education*
Jane Jacomb-Hood *Sponsorship*
Brenda Leedham *Wigs and Make-up*
William Lockwood *Property Shop*
Nigel Loomes *Paint Shop*
Peter Pullinger *Construction*
Frances Roe *Wardrobe*
John Watts *Safety*
Guy Woolfenden *Music*

Swan Theatre
Tamsin Thomas *Press (0789) 296655*
Peter Cholerton *Property Master*
Mark Collins *Master Carpenter*
Sonja Dosanjh *Company Manager*
Wayne Dowdeswell *Chief Electrician*
Brian Glover *RSC Collection*
Josie Horton *Deputy Wardrobe Mistress*
Geoff Locker *Production Manager*
Chris Neale *House Manager*
Richard Power *Deputy Chief Electrician*
Eileen Relph *House Manager*
Richard Rhodes *Deputy Theatre Manager*
Emma Romer *Publicity*
Graham Sawyer *Theatre Manager and Licensee*
Ursula Selbiger *Box Office Manager*
Michael Tubbs *Director of Music*
John Woolf *Music Director*

Production Credits for The Man of Mode
Scenery, painting, properties, costumes and wigs made in RST Workshops, Stratford-upon-Avon. Additional costumes made by Doreen Brown and Kate Wyatt. Swan Property Manager Mark Graham. Fans from Neal St. East; glasses from David Mellor. Thanks to Francine Watson-Coleman for advice on Restoration movement.

Facilities
In addition to bar and coffee facilities on the ground floor, there is wine on sale on the first floor bridge outside Gallery 1. Toilets, including facilities for disabled people, are situated on the ground floor only.

RSC Collection
Over a thousand items on view: costumes, props, pictures and sound recordings illustrating the changes in staging from medieval times to the use of the thrust stage in the Swan, and comparisons of past productions of the current season's plays. Come and see our exhibition; browse in the sales and refreshments area – and book a backstage tour. Open from 9.15am. Sundays from 12.00.

'The Man of Mode':
a Critical Commentary
by Simon Trussler

The Compiler

Simon Trussler has contributed the commentaries to ten previous volumes in Methuen's Swan Theatre Plays series. He has been an editor of *New Theatre Quarterly* and its predecessor *Theatre Quarterly* since 1971, and presently teaches in the Drama Department of Goldsmiths' College, University of London. *Shakespearean Concepts*, due from Methuen London in 1989, will be the latest of nearly two-dozen books on theatrical subjects he has written or edited, and he was also founding-editor of the Royal Shakespeare Company's *Yearbook* in 1978, compiling the annual editions until 1985.

Synopsis

Dorimant, in the process of discarding one mistress, Mrs Loveit, while trying to seduce Bellinda, learns of the arrival in town of the heiress Harriet, accompanied by her suspicious mother, Lady Woodvill. He is soon joined by his man-about-town friend, the gossipy Medley, and by the honourable Young Bellair, whose hopes of winning the hand of the virtuous Emilia are threatened by his father's plans to marry him to Harriet. Dorimant, hoping to disengage himself from Mrs Loveit, pretends jealousy of the flamboyant Sir Fopling Flutter, whose self-opinionated attentions Mrs Loveit at first encourages in order to discountenance Dorimant before Medley. After tricking his way into Lady Woodvill's confidence in disguise, Dorimant pays his addresses to Harriet, whose knowing wit and fortune he finds equally agreeable: but he still seizes the opportunity to tempt Bellinda into bed at his lodgings — from which her early-morning departure threatens multiple disclosures. Following the secret marriage of Emilia to Young Bellair, not only the bridegroom's deceived father but also the impressionable Lady Woodvill are reconciled to the choices of their offspring, and Dorimant agrees to woo Harriet respectably in Hampshire — though not before seeking a further assignation with Bellinda, and achieving the public humiliation of Mrs Loveit, who repudiates the unsnubbable Sir Fopling and departs cursing the entire company.

Stage History

The first known performance of *The Man of Mode* took place on 11 March 1676, at the recently-opened theatre in Dorset Garden. Its cast included all the leading players in the Duke's company, whose joint managers since Davenant's death, Thomas Betterton and Henry Harris, took the roles of Dorimant and Medley. The protean William Smith created the part of Sir Fopling Flutter, while Mary Betterton played Bellinda, and the greatest tragic actress of the age, Elizabeth Barry, became the most renowned Mrs Loveit, though it is uncertain whether she was the first.

A letter to Etherege during his absence abroad in 1685 records of a court performance that 'Sir Fopling appeared with the usual applause', confirming that the play was already a favourite in the repertoire, and by the time records become a little less scanty in the early eighteenth century, *The Man of Mode* was being revived around three times each season, with Robert Wilks a favourite as Dorimant, at first opposite the Harriet of Anne Bracegirdle, whose younger rival Anne Oldfield made the role of Mrs Loveit her own. The veteran comic player William Penkethman took on the role of Old Bellair, while Colley Cibber was an inevitable Sir Fopling. He was followed in the part by his son Theophilus in the 1730s, but by this time the play was already becoming less popular, and a performance in 1755 was said to have been 'much disliked and hissed'. The last recorded revival in the eighteenth century took place on 15 March 1766.

Although the Prospect Theatre Company opened a touring revival at the Georgian Theatre in Richmond, Yorkshire, in 1965, the first modern London production was by Terry Hands in 1971, for the Royal Shakespeare Company at the Aldwych Theatre, when Alan Howard played Dorimant opposite the Loveit of Vivien Merchant, the Bellinda of Frances de la Tour, and the Harriet of Helen Mirren, while John Wood took the role of Sir Fopling Flutter. 'Restoration drama doesn't appear to have been the kind of finger-twirling mannered performance we've become used to', declared Terry Hands, who transposed the play into a near-contemporary setting. In 1984 came another modern-dress production at the Orange Tree Theatre, directed by Sam Walters, in which Tom Georgeson played Dorimant, Christina Greatrex took the role of Mrs Loveit, and David Timson that of Sir Fopling. The Cheek by Jowl company then revived the play, in a touring version which reached the Donmar Warehouse Theatre in London in March 1986, where it played almost in-the-round. In this production, directed by Declan Donnellan, Martin Turner was Dorimant, Anne White was Mrs Loveit, Saskia Reeves was Harriet, and David Gillespie played Sir Fopling.

Sir George Etherege: a Brief Chronology

1635 *c.* Born, eldest son among the seven children of Captain George Etherege and Mary Powney, shortly after his father's return from the Bermudas, where his grandfather owned extensive property.

1636 His father purchased a place at court, as Purveyor to Queen Henrietta Maria.

1644 Presumably joined his parents when they followed Henrietta Maria into exile in Paris during the Civil Wars.

1650 Death of his father in France. An unproven tradition has it that Etherege was attending Lord Williams's Grammar School at Thame. He was now in the care of his grandfather.

1654 Possibly after travelling in France and Flanders, became articled clerk to a lawyer who practised in Beaconsfield and in London.

1658 Death of his grandfather, whose estates he inherited after some legal wrangling.

1659 Entered Clement's Inn as a law student. His activities until 1663 uncertain, although by then he was already on familiar terms with Lord Buckhurst, and apparently established in courtly circles. Over the next few years became intimate with the 'Restoration court wits', notably Buckhurst, Rochester, and Sedley.

1664 Successful first performance of *The Comical Revenge; or, Love in a Tub*, by the Duke's Men at their theatre in Lincoln's Inn Fields, probably in March or April, and two editions published in the same year.

1668 *She Would If She Could* first performed on 6 February, again by the Duke's Men at Lincoln's Inn Fields, and published in the same year. Appointed as a Gentleman of the Privy Chamber in Ordinary. Sent on diplomatic mission to Constantinople as secretary to the Ambassador Extraordinary, Sir Daniel Harvey.

1671 Returned from Constantinople, via Paris, and resumed a courtly life of leisured and sometimes quarrelsome affluence. Involved in a duel with Colonel Ashton in September.

1676 11 March, first recorded performance of *The Man of Mode* by the Duke's Men at their new theatre in Dorset Garden. Present at Epsom in July during a brawl with the watch which resulted in the death of his and Rochester's companion, Captain Downes. By this time, in the service of Mary of Modena, the Duchess of York.

1677 Involved in a tavern brawl with a fellow-courtier, the pugnacious Henry Bulkeley.

1678 *c.* Marriage, to the 'rich old widow', Mary Sheppard Arnold, who, according to anecdote, insisted on his purchase of a knighthood. The marriage was not successful.

1682 Given a pension by the heir apparent, the Duke of York.

1685 Death of Charles II, and accession of his Catholic brother as James II. Etherege, after years of some obscurity during which he was said to be gambling addictively, sent (without his wife) as Resident to the Imperial Court of Ratisbon in Bavaria. An avid correspondent with his friends during his three years there, he was also allegedly converted to Catholicism, and scandalized his protocol-obsessed fellow-diplomats by an open affair with an itinerant actress.

1688 The 'bloodless revolution' deposed James II, whom Etherege followed into exile in France in the following year.

1692 Death, presumably in Paris, on or about 10 May. Collected *Works* published posthumously, 1704.

The Altered Face of the Stage

When play-acting returned to London with the Restoration, after being banned by the puritans since 1642, it was at first in improvised theatres, converted from 'real' (or 'royal') indoor tennis courts. Of the two companies granted royal patents, the King's Men, under the management of Thomas Killigrew, was the first to move to a purpose-built playhouse, the Theatre Royal in Bridges Street, Drury Lane, in 1663. But the second company, the Duke of York's, under the management of Sir William Davenant, continued to play in the converted Lisle's Tennis Court in Lincoln's Inn Fields, and it was here that Etherege's first two plays, *The Comical Revenge* and *She Would If She Could*, were first performed, in 1664 and 1668. Three years later, the Duke's Men moved to their own new playhouse, designed by Sir Christopher Wren, situated in Dorset Garden (alongside the Thames and not far from the city wall), where *The Man of Mode* reached the stage in 1676. Meanwhile, the King's Men had taken over at Lincoln's Inn Fields following the destruction of their own playhouse by fire in 1672, until a new Drury Lane theatre, also built to Wren's designs, was ready for occupation some two years later.

Looking back nostalgically to the Restoration years in 1725, John Dennis remarked that 'They alter'd at once the whole face of the stage by introducing scenes and women'. This was only half true: the court masques of the Jacobean and Caroline period had employed some elaborate scenery, and the open-air theatres of the Elizabethans had long been giving way to indoor 'private' theatres, with greater potential for technical effects. The difference now was that the proscenium arch formed a 'picture-frame' for the painted perspective scenery, changed by the wings-and-shutters system, which provided a formalized background to Restoration comedy and tragedy.

But it was *only* a background: the actors performed on the extensive apron stage in front of the proscenium, in a relationship with their audiences no less intimate and uncluttered than their forebears. Indeed, Restoration theatres, which seated from around five to eight hundred, were actually smaller than the Elizabethan public playhouses, and their audiences, although not drawn quite so exclusively from a courtly elite as has sometimes been suggested, certainly felt themselves to be part of a social as much as of a theatrical occasion.

With just two companies of less than thirty players apiece, acting was thus an exclusive though not prestigious profession, its members as well-known personally to many in the audience as their acquaintances in the pit or boxes. And, although the patents stressed that the introduction of actresses was a matter of morality — to correct the abuse of men appearing 'in the habits of women' — the intimacy between these players and their audiences was not confined to closeness in the auditorium. It was probably inevitable that, in the absence of a traditional route for women into the profession, some actresses in a licentious age should have achieved their positions through sexual patronage — though it is also indisputable that Elizabeth Barry, despite her path being smoothed by the notorious rake Lord Rochester, became a remarkable tragic actress (and a notable Mrs Loveit besides) while Nell Gwyn, although she owed her early chances to being the mistress of a prominent player, Charles Hart, became no less striking a comic actress before she caught the eye of the king.

Other actresses, such as the great Thomas Betterton's wife Mary (Etherege's first Bellinda), were nonetheless able to lead lives of untainted virtue at a time when such behaviour in courtly society was almost eccentric — while the fine comic actress Anne Bracegirdle (whose roles included Harriet in *The Man of Mode*) even managed to sustain a reputation for excessive prudishness in private life. This did not, however, prevent her being thought fair game for predatory males: as late as 1692, an assault on her honour was compounded by the murder of the actor William Mountford, who had tried to intervene on her behalf. Those guilty were not severely punished.

When *The Man of Mode* reached the stage in 1676, the canon of Restoration drama destined to survive in the repertoire of the modern theatre included, apart from the work of Etherege and Wycherley, just one or two seldom-revived pieces by Dryden, Otway, and Aphra Behn. Vanbrugh and Congreve were mere schoolboys, George Farquhar not even born. Within a couple of years, in 1678, the 'popish plot' was to distract royal attention from theatrical matters, and by 1682 playgoing had so far declined that the King's and Duke's men merged to form a single 'united company', which was found sufficient for London's theatrical needs for the following thirteen years. Arguably, if there ever was a distinctive mode of 'Restoration comedy' it was, even from the first, slightly 'out of sync' with the mood of the society it reflected, and of the court and the courtiers from whom its patronage and its audiences largely derived. But if any single playwright can be properly identified with the mode, and even credited with its creation, that playwright was surely Sir George Etherege.

The 'Noble Idleness' of Gentle George

While wit opened many doors along the galleries of Whitehall Palace, where the restored King Charles held court, it could not have been expected to close the gap between the noble amateurs and those who, though often intimate with the courtly circle, needed to write for their livings. The most notable of these professionals included the much underrated latter-day Jonsonian, Thomas Shadwell, besides the man who so savagely lampooned his erstwhile companion in the satirical poem *MacFlecknoe*, but lost the laureateship to him in 1689, John Dryden. Shadwell wrote in all some twenty plays and operas, while Dryden was even more prolific as a dramatist, despite his greater posthumous fame as critic and poet.

This is not the place to investigate the equivocal relationship between such professionals and the gentlemen courtiers who wrote for fame and fun: but one easily measurable distinction is, quite simply, that the 'amateurs' were far less prolific. And among those of any lasting literary interest, George Etherege achieved an output even slenderer than that of the notoriously indolent George Villiers, Duke of Buckingham. But whereas Buckingham was, in Dryden's judgement, 'everything by starts, and nothing long', and to a degree made up in virtuosity what he lacked in staying power, Etherege really had few other strings to his bow, despite his occasional forays into foreign diplomacy. His letters back home from these trips form, indeed, the fullest surviving correspondence of any Restoration dramatist, and — aside from some acutely undistinguished verse — are Etherege's only other claim to literary fame.

Dryden was one of Etherege's correspondents during his years in Ratisbon in the service of James II, and in a letter of 1687 the loyal laureate regrets the new king's capacity for stirring up controversy. 'Oh that our Monarch would encourage noble idleness', he bemoans, with only a trace of irony, 'as he of blessed memory did before him, for my mind misgives me that he will not much advance his affairs by stirring.' The prescience here aside, the nostalgia for Charles's encouragement of 'noble idleness' catches exactly the air of self-conscious (and utterly self-confident) insouciance which Dryden himself could only vicariously cultivate, but which Etherege, thanks to his grandfather's investments and his father's procurement of a place at court, almost came to personify.

No wonder, then, that Etherege is often credited with the 'invention' of the so-called 'comedy of manners', that dramatic reflection of the upper-class lifestyle of Restoration London, of which even Wycherley — as *The Plain Dealer*, in particular, amply affirms — felt himself an often critical observer. Even Sir Charles Sedley (quite apart from his lack of comparable distinction as a dramatist), gives the impression of having led altogether too *busy* a life to have been quite so resoundingly representative of 'noble idleness' as 'easy Etherege' —or, as his alternative, no-less-alliterative soubriquet described him, 'gentle George'. And whereas the four comedies of 'brawny Wycherley' were written over a mere five-year span (and his theatrical career would surely have continued but for the debilitating illness which struck him so soon after), Etherege's total output amounted to just three plays over twelve years. From then on, despite the urgent pleadings of his fellow-wits and apparently even of the king, 'play' for Etherege meant a vent ure at the card table. Indeed, the indulgence of this weakness — along with the pursuit of his 'strongest passion', the fair sex — now became his chief employment. As he frankly confessed, 'I have preferred my pleasure to my profit'.

Etherege's earliest play, *The Comical Revenge; or, Love in a Tub,* had been written in 1664, presumably by way of establishing his rightful place among the wits of the recently-restored court, and in this it evidently succeeded. Pepys's description is tantalizing: *Love in a Tub*, he wrote, 'is very merry, but only so by gesture, not wit at all'. The piece blends a serious, 'heroic' love plot, duly couched in rhyming couplets, with no less than three levels of comic action, involving the pursuit of a rich widow, the misadventures of a pox-ridden French valet, and the gulling of a country knight. Such pleasure as the play can still give lies in its very profusion of action and invention — and its importance in capturing, however tentatively, a tone of voice which is so distinctively of its time, particularly in the scenes of verbalized sexual combat between the rakish Sir Frederick and the knowing, witty Widow Rich.

She Would If She Could came four years later, in 1668, in the midst of the vogue for heroic drama. Its title refers to the aspirations of its central character, Lady Cockwood, to manage simultaneously her appetite for men and her honour — and the thwarting of her desire for the otherwise no-less-aptly named hero, Courtall. Particularly in vituperative vein, she dominates the two couples whose love passages are more successful, and who are duly affianced at the end of the play. Whether these matches will stand the test of time and temptation is left as carefully ambiguous as Dorimant's ability to find lasting happiness in Hampshire at the climax of *The Man of Mode*. For this, which was also to be his last play, the town had to wait another eight years. And then, at the moment of his greatest triumph, 'easy' Etherege laid down his pen.

A Philosophy Fit for a King

Amidst the rakes, wits, and libertines of Charles's court was to be found an honoured octogenarian who had been tutor to the king in his years in exile, and who was still favoured by the restored monarch for his company and conversation — the philosopher Thomas Hobbes. His most important work, the *Leviathan*, had offended royalists no less than puritans on its first publication in 1651: but it offered, now, such persuasive support for the king's absolutist ambitions and for the self-aggrandisement of his followers that the prevalent pursuit of pleasure became almost a scientific duty. By the turn of the century, it was unacceptable creatures such as Vizard in Farquhar's *The Constant Couple* who were turning to Hobbes to justify their behaviour: but in the 1670s Etherege's Dorimant was able to remain a hero as well as a selfish hedonist in the true Hobbesian mould. Such, claimed Hobbes, was the nature of man.

Whereas his Parisian acquaintance Descartes had conceived matter and soul as different kinds of reality, Hobbes declared that consciousness itself was not separable from but simply a response to the motions of external matter. And even this seemingly abstract concept was ultimately bound up with Hobbes's political beliefs: for faith in the *independent* existence of the soul, and so in the world of spirits and of priestly power over them, was, he claimed, among those many 'things that serve to lessen the dependence of subjects on the sovereign power of their country' — in short, to weaken their allegiance to their king. This somewhat tortuous argument in favour of a strong monarchy no doubt answered Hobbes's own deepest desires for security from the vicissitudes of civil conflict: but substituting the sovereign for the soul also made Hobbes the earliest English philosopher of materialism, though it was not yet so-called.

Hobbes's belief that the ruling factors in men's actions were the pursuit of personal pleasure and the avoidance of pain made his philosophy also fundamentally determinist: for he held that, however we may persuade ourselves that we are exercising free will in deciding our actions, we are in fact only responding to external stimuli by 'choosing' what is best calculated to achieve pleasure or circumvent pain. And if men can only act according to the pressures of external events, good and evil themselves become no more than appetites and aversions which we cannot but strive to pursue or circumvent.

In a passage worth quoting at length for its expression of the gist of Hobbes's philosophy, as of the spirit of the Restoration court and its comedy, Hobbes seems to liken human life to a race in which one never reaches the finishing post:

To endeavour is appetite: to be remiss is sensuality: to consider them behind is glory: to consider them before is humility: . . . .to fall on a sudden is disposition to weep: to see another fall is disposition to laugh: to see one outgone whom we would not, is pity: to see one outgo whom we would not, is indignation: to hold fast by another is love: to carry him on that so holdeth is charity: to hurt oneself for haste is shame: . . . continually to be outgone is misery: continually to outgo the next before is felicity: and to forsake the course is to die.

When the Anglican divine, Jeremy Collier, came in 1698 to launch his influential attack upon Restoration comedy in *A Short View of the Immorality and Profaneness of the English Stage*, he objected to the titillating effects of its many sexual chases, in which 'Tis not the success, but the manner of gaining it which is all in all'. That, of course, was precisely Hobbes's point: happiness lies in the aspiration rather than the achievement. Dorimant is thus driven by the *pursuit* of pleasure, which is necessarily selfish: for, as Hobbes puts it, 'seeing all delight is appetite, and presupposeth a further end, there can be no contentment but in proceeding'.

Hobbes argued that such an uncontrolled conflict of self-interests would, in the natural condition of mankind, result in war and destruction. And so man had constructed his Leviathan — that ingenious automaton 'called the Commonwealth or State', an 'artificial man . . . of greater stature and strength than the natural, for whose protection and defence it was intended'. The sovereign, whose authority must be absolute, thus controls the body-politic. Men surrender their freedom to avoid their destruction, and the 'race', as Restoration comedy reflects, goes to the sexually speedy instead of the politically ambitious.

The Restoration wits were cultivated men who read their *Leviathan* as well as rubbing shoulders at court with its author. How far they were men of appetite who found pleasure it its philosophical justification of their desires, how far the philosophical justification acted as an aphrodisiac to the appetite, is now impossible to judge. Hobbes made a curiously English marriage between the laid-back pleasure-principle long since embedded in Epicurean philosophy, and the aggressive political pragmatism advocated by Machiavelli. So too, it seems, did the sovereign he once taught, and who now honoured him with a pension in his old age — though in the opinion of the contemporary historian Bishop Burnet, Charles himself was too lazy to be a successfully despotic ruler in the true Hobbesian mould. He, like his courtiers, preferred the no less Hobbesian pursuit of pleasure.

Writers and Critics on Etherege

To speak plainly of this whole work, I think nothing but being lost to a sense of innocence and virtue can make anyone see this comedy without observing more frequent occasion to move sorrow and indignation than mirth and laughter. At the same time I allow it to be nature, but it is nature in its utmost corruption and degeneracy.

Richard Steele (1711)

But can anything but corrupt and degenerate nature be the proper subject of comedy? And can anything but ridicule be the proper subject of comedy?

John Dennis (1722)

You see there to what insults a woman of wit, beauty, and quality is exposed that has been seduced by the artificial tenderness of a vain agreeable gallant; and I believe that very comedy has given more checks to ladies in pursuit of present pleasures, so closely attended with shame and sorrow, than all the sermons they ever heard in their lives.

Lady Mary Wortley Montagu (1746)

Take one of their characters, male or female (with very few exceptions they are all alike), and place it in a modern play, and my virtuous indignation shall rise against the profligate wretch as warmly as the Catos of the pit, because in a modern play I am to judge of right and wrong.... But in its own world do we feel the creature is so very bad? The Fainalls and the Mirabells, the Dorimants and the Lady Touchwoods, in their own sphere, do not offend my moral sense.... They have got out of Christendom into the land of — what shall I call it? — the Utopia of gallantry, where pleasure is duty, and the manner perfect freedom.

Charles Lamb (1823)

Etherege, if you will, is a minor writer, in his exuberance nearer Mrs Behn than to Congreve with his depth. But from another point of view he is far above all the other playwrights of the period, for he did something very rare in our literature. He presented life treated purely as an appearance.... Here is no sense of grappling with circumstance, for man is unencumbered by thoughts or passions. Life is a merry-go-round, and there is no need to examine the machinery or ponder on the design.

Bonamy Dobrée (1924)

As for Dorimant, his head is unquestionably better than his heart, and the modern reader must resign himself to a world which held that its Loveits and Bellindas could not eat their cake and have it too. An amour is pleasant, but when it ceases to be pleasant, it is broken off as a matter of course.

H.F.B. Brett-Smith (1927)

It seems to me that what the play provides — apart from the briskly handled intrigue — is a demonstration of the physical stamina of Dorimant. But Miss Lynch sees further. For her, Dorimant is 'the fine flowering of Restoration culture.... We laugh at Dorimant because his assumed affectation admits of so poor and incomplete an expression of an attractive and vigorous personality.' The 'unfailing grace and distinction' are perhaps not much in evidence in Dorimant's treatment of Mrs Loveit; but even if we ignore these brutish scenes, we are forced to ask, how do we know that there *is* this 'attractive and vigorous personality' beneath the conventional forms? Dorimant's intrigues are of no more human significance than those of a barnyard cock.

L.C. Knights (1937)

The comedy of love, of nature and art, of wit, passion, and control is everywhere conditioned by this comedy of manners. The comedy has, of course, those other facets which we have inspected — in the hero, the libertine-Machiavel beneath the manners of the honest man; in the world of Lady Townley, the capacity of manners to corrupt their own value and the value of a sanctioned morality which they in other ways express. But the final comedy of both concerns is that the society of the play, whether it pursues pleasure or power, does so in an endless and sterile round of play houses, parks, drawing rooms, and 'all the little news o' the town'.

Dale Underwood (1957)

Here are the love duel, the fop, the libertine, the conflict between generations, the oppositions of country and town, of England and France — in short, almost all the themes and characters that we associate with the tradition of Restoration comedy. Etherege's treatment of characters, in particular, sets a standard by which to measure the tradition as a whole.... Sir Fopling, Dorimant, and Harriet claim our attention equally. None triumphs as a dramatic character at the expense of another. It is to them, especially, that *The Man of Mode* owes its representative quality.

W.B. Carnochan (1967)

The Art and Craft of Affectation

The Man of Mode is replete with the kinds of characters who were to become conventional in Restoration comedy — several of whom had, for that matter, already been introduced by such Caroline dramatists as James Shirley. The Darwinian breed of dramatic critic has duly dug out direct ancestors in the play for most of the types allegedly brought to evolutionary perfection at the end of the century by Congreve in *The Way of the World* — in which the female characters do, admittedly, seem uncannily congruent with Loveit, Bellinda, and Harriet in their relationships with their respective rakish heroes. And wasn't Congreve's close contemporary Vanbrugh busy elevating the Fopling Flutters of the 1690s into his own (and Colley Cibber's) Lord Foppington? But this sort of evolutionary approach tends to ignore an essential missing link — which is the common descent of these types not just from dramatic antecedents but from life.

When Charles Lamb apologetically defended Restoration comedy on the grounds that it was 'artificial', he spoke more truly than he knew: for so far from such plays being the products of the dramatists' dream worlds, their very 'artifice' was a reflection of the milieu of a social elite which lived according to its own code of quasi-theatrical conventions. Thus, when Emilia asks Medley in *The Man of Mode* for examples of the 'new wit', he recommends to her not songs or novels, as she expects, but two guidebooks to correct behaviour, to one of which he gives the title *The Art of Affectation*. Etherege's editors have identified the original of this as a popular work published in the previous year, *The Gentlewoman's Companion* , whose purpose was, precisely, to teach young ladies how to 'perform' in high society.

Behaviour in *The Man of Mode* is consistently conceived as theatrical, or in terms of performing roles: and it is, interestingly, not Dorimant but the virtuous and significantly-named Bellair who gives Harriet, fresh from the country, her lesson in pretending to be in love with him — which he finally applauds as 'admirably well acted'. Much of this acting lesson of Harriet's has to do with the many ways of holding her fan — a visual aid to social and sexual discourse of considerable.subtlety, since its signals could variously affirm, contradict, or modulate the spoken word. In *The Spectator*, Addison later imagined a mock-academy for 'handling the fan', whose syllabus would cover the many ways of tapping, opening, unfurling, discharging, and fluttering' a fan — this latter exercise including the making of fine distinctions between angry, modest, timorous, confused, merry, and amorous emotions. So what Mrs Loveit is 'saying' when, almost inconceivably, she 'tears her fan in pieces' in *The Man of Mode* is clearly only half-expressed by the 'hell and furies' she flings verbally at Dorimant.

In his illuminating study of *Restoration Theatre Production*, the late Jocelyn Powell cited many examples from seventeenth-century sources to illustrate the theory attributed by Charles Gildon to Thomas Betterton, the greatest actor of his age and Etherege's first Dorimant:

Every passion or emotion of the mind has from nature its proper and peculiar countenance, sound, and gesture; and the whole body of man, all his looks, and every sound of his voice, like the strings of an instrument, receive their sounds from the various impulses of the passions.

Betterton, of course, was describing an approach to acting: but many books of the period offer instruction which derives no less clearly from the belief that everyday behaviour — with all its recurrent ceremonies of greeting and parting, bowing and complimenting, asserting or acknowledging precedence, and modes of signifying sexual alertness —is best governed by such conventionalized forms of expression. Even facial emotions were supposedly classifiable according to the exact physiognomic rules formulated by Charles Lebrun.

Sir Fopling Flutter, we note, arrives at Lady Townley's fresh from 'the king's *couchée*': even the royal preparations for going to bed were, indeed, part of the ceremonial social round, a sort of performance. And masters of such ceremonies might perform a similar role in the theatre: as Powell points out, in an age long before theatre directors were thought of, but when playwrights were far less immediately involved in the rehearsal process than in Shakespeare's day, the dancing-master was almost certainly prominent in 'designing' the tableaux of a play, and probably also helped with the groupings — as when characters 'come forward', 'retire', or 'converse apart'. Wycherley showed a disguised young lover in effect doing just that in *The Gentleman Dancing Master*: and the consequent confusion of levels of reality — with a real dancing-master no doubt instructing the actor how simultaneously to be and to pretend to be a dancing-master — was only stretching to its comic limits that long hall of mirrors through which Restoration audiences watched Restoration actors playing people very much like themselves. No wonder looking-glasses figure so prominently in *The Man of Mode* — and no wonder that generations of scholars have played the game of trying to identify the 'real-life' originals of its characters. Whether Dorimant was 'really' Rochester or Dorset or Monmouth or even Etherege himself doesn't much matter: that he *might* have been any or all of them surely does.

The Sexual Lore of the Libertines

Upper-class women in Restoration London suffered from the worst aspects of their own society's hypocrisy and a typology of their sex which was much more traditional. The female orgasm, so far from being the discreet unmentionable it had become by Victorian times, was regarded as the reason for women's alleged carnality, and Aphra Behn was merely echoing a commonplace when she suggested in 1682 that the demands of young wives for multiple orgasms were often responsible for the sexual exhaustion of their husbands. So readily were women allegedly given to sexual arousal that the married male needed to strike a delicate balance between leaving his wife frustrated and over-stimulated — both conditions supposedly leading to a lover's bed. Yet the husband, too, was warned against over-passionate conjugal love, for nothing was 'more impure than to love a wife like an adulterous woman'. Having legitimate children was, after all, primarily intended to secure one's lineage, and while it was therefore allowable for males to sire bastards, the threat to the proper descent of one's estate of being cuckolded unknowingly was even more to be feared than the slur on one's honour of being a complaisant wittol in the public eye.

The 'double standard' thus arose not because men's need for sexual activity permitted them freedoms of which women were thought to have no need, but because the potential promiscuity of women made it necessary to protect both masculine honour and the laws of primogeniture by the strictest control over female sexuality. This had, ironically, been seriously questioned only by the puritans, who not only advocated an equality of the sexes within 'holy matrimony', but held that sex outside marriage was, if no better, at least no worse for women than for men. The true royalist thus restored the 'double standard' along with the king, as a matter of religion and loyalty as well as of personal convenience. But in practice the sexual freedom for which the Restoration court became notorious, and which certainly permeates much Restoration comedy, imposed even greater constraints on women. At one extreme, virginity — no longer protected by the catholic veneration for the Virgin Mary and by the respect due to those who felt called to be nuns — was, beyond a 'certain age', a matter for ridicule. But, as Etherege's Lady Cockwood and Mrs Loveit exemplify, women who actually practised sexual freedom as active agents rather than passive receptacles were no less destined to be the objects of male disgust, once they had ceased to be the objects of arousal. In any event, only the well-endowed widow — traditionally the fairest game of all — was in a position of sufficient economic independence to support any genuine kind of female sexual freedom.

All this was further complicated by the tradition of the arranged marriage. Scholarly debate continues over how far the so-called 'affective marriage' was becoming the norm rather than the exception in the higher echelons of society: in the drama, at least, fathers were still busily trying to force sons into marriages of dynastic or economic convenience, while themselves, in effect, purchasing younger wives to replace those who had either died in childbirth or from sheer exhaustion. Old Bellair in *The Man of Mode* does not succeed in such plans — but in this respect Etherege's comedy is highly traditional, tracing youth's eternal triumph over age in defiance of most experience. In other respects, the piece is more of its own sexual moment, showing Dorimant successfully humiliating the 'insatiable' Loveit, successfully seducing the 'sexually free' Bellinda — but actually marrying the heiress Harriet, who, because this is a play, happens also to be witty and beautiful.

The first we hear of Harriet is thus from the Orange-Woman, who defines precisely her necessary qualities — 'there are few finer women . . . and a hugeous fortune they say'. And Dorimant elsewhere elevates expedience into a sententious rhymed tag, spoken to Young Bellair:

The wise will find a difference in our fate,
You wed a woman, I a good estate.

And even Mrs Loveit finds that 'my grief hangs lighter on my soul' when Dorimant explains to her that he needs a wife 'to repair the ruins of my estate'. There is, incidentally, no sign of a Mr Loveit, so it must be assumed either that Mrs Loveit is a widow or that she has taken the title (as did Restoration actresses) as a mark of respectability. In that case, there are no married couples in *The Man of Mode* — apart from the peripheral Shoemaker, who says he 'lives like a gentleman' with his wife: 'I never mind her motions, she never inquires into mine, we speak to one another civilly, hate one another heartily, and because 'tis vulgar to lie and soak together, we have each of us our several settle-bed.' This sums up well enough the supposed state of conjugal misery earlier illustrated by Etherege in the Cockwoods of *She Would If She Could*.

It is a frequent paradox of Restoration comedy that its younger characters are so often shown aspiring plotfully to a state shown by its older characters to be a certain cause of mutual unhappiness. Dorimant, of course, recognizes the dangers, and is already holding Bellinda in readiness to alleviate the tedium of married bliss. The combination of honesty and hypocrisy in his action is typical enough — as is his lack of real sexual self-knowledge.

Dorimant and the Restoration Drones

The first of the many mistresses brought by King Charles to Whitehall was Barbara Palmer, later Duchess of Cleveland. She came, asserts one historian — illustrating his belief from Andrew Marvell's none-too-coy poem about her sharing her bath with a passing footman — 'as close to nymphomania as makes no matter'. Not unexpectedly, the same historian makes no such quasi-medical diagnosis of the king's own sexual appetite, as he lists the fallen housemaids alongside the courtesans-cum-duchesses who shared the royal bed. It is not, he hastens to reassure us, that more sex went on in Whitehall than at the discreet French court of Louis XIV or even, he surmises, in the Vatican: simply, the English were less hypocritical about it, and conducted their amorous adventures in the open — indeed, we might add, assimilated them into the prevailing culture. The line was certainly a thin one between the sexual directness (not to mention the *doubles entendres*) permitted in the performed plays and published poems of the time, and the obscenities reserved for 'private' circulation — whose authors, were of course, the same.

Barbara Palmer not only led a sexual life of her own, she also had an independent mind and a quick temper. And of all Charles's mistresses she was accordingly the most disliked by the male courtiers. Although a cousin to the notorious Rochester, she was nevertheless a target for his vicious poetic lampoons, in one of which he typically complains:

Full forty men a day provided for this whore,
Yet like a bitch she wags her tail for more.

And in 'Signior Dildo' Rochester extended his fire to include a round dozen of courtly ladies supposedly devoted to the helpful signior's assistance.

It is easy enough for literary critics to 'place' such poems within a lyric tradition, less so for the theatre historian seeking a context for a case-study in sexual attraction-repulsion such as *The Man of Mode*. Earlier, Etherege's poetic attack on that best-natured of the king's mistresses, and softest of satirical targets, Nell Gwyn, had itself been embedded within his first play, *The Comical Revenge*: but if he was generally a less vocal woman-hater than Rochester, that was probably due to his laziness rather than his enlightenment. His last two plays both pose the problem of how to 'place' Restoration misogyny within Restoration comedy. In particular, how are we to understand the roles of such sexually-assertive women as Lady Cockwood in *She Would If She Could* and — the name's almost the same — Mrs Loveit in *The Man of Mode*?

Most critics have tended to avoid or ignore the issue. So Mrs Loveit is regarded simply as a 'dupe', inferior to Dorimant in her capacity for plotting because, unlike her erstwhile lover, she cannot bring her passions under control. In this light, she may indeed be viewed as a less efficient Hobbesian than Dorimant: in the light of even the most tolerant feminist critique, however, she may also be seen as a typical figment of male fantasy, her eventual downfall representing a masculine triumph over her independent sexuality. Courtall in *She Would if She Could*, normally as promiscuous by name as by nature, despises the one woman who 'would if she could' no less assiduously than Dorimant despises Mrs Loveit — or than the male courtiers of Whitehall despised the assertive Barbara Palmer.

So it is highly appropriate that in *The Man of Mode* the one woman whom Dorimant is actually willing to marry should be Harriet — in the conventional terms he himself acknowledges, because she has both wealth and beauty, but surely no less because she is the least sexually demanding or responsive woman in the play — rather like that long line of Wodehousian heroines whose greatest virtue is that they will make some member of the Drones Club a jolly good chum. The comparison is not that far-fetched: for Wodehouse's world of the gentleman's club, of gentlemen's gentlemen, and of the indolent social calendar of the idle rich is, within its own chronological terms, not so very far from Etherege's. It is in one respect also more honest, for Wodehouse's Bertie Woosters and Freddie Widgeons and Bingo Littles at least *knew* that they were afraid of any woman not androgynously like themselves. It is the Dorimants (and the Rochesters and the Etheredges of the Restoration court) who needed to sublimate their fear through an interminable succession of sexual conquests, and to celebrate these in poems of vituperative disgust — with women and with themselves.

All this continued to be conventionalized in the drama long after 'liberated' sexuality had ceased to characterize the court. Even Mirabell in Congreve's *The Way of the World* prefers the bantering chumminess of Millamant to the lingering potency of Fainall, and as for the much-vaunted 'equality' of the contract he makes with her, isn't it in essence a response to the cry of the Henry Higginses down the ages — why can't a woman be more like a man? Harriet in *The Man of Mode* is, of course, just that, and Brian Gibbons accordingly believes that 'the play shows Harriet in the process of moving across the threshold into full adulthood' — though, revealingly, he proceeds to declare that her contemplation of marriage is an 'expression of reckless competitiveness, with Dorimant and with her female rivals'. And Dale Underwood claims her for the heroine 'because she has sufficient wit and self-control to withstand the assault of the hero and to hold out . . . for marriage'. To Gibbons's 'masculine' virtue of competitiveness Underwood thus adds the qualities of self-control and manipulation — also presumably regarded as signs of 'moving across the threshold into full adulthood'.

Dorimant does nothing disinterestedly. He favours the marriage between Young Bellair and Emilia from the first, but solely on the grounds that 'nothing can corrupt her but a husband' — and maybe the good opinion Emilia begins to hold of him anticipates even her eventual surrender. Of course, it is as fallacious to project a world of events and consequences beyond the final curtain as it is unhistorical to expect Dorimant or Harriet — or Etherege — to transcend their own socio-theatrical circumstances. Yet Etherege chooses to end his play on an equivocal note, so that even the single accomplished marriage, of Emilia and Young Bellair, may be seen as part of the longer-term sexual planning on which we see Dorimant musing in the first act.

Meanwhile, there are the antics of Sir Fopling Flutter to sweeten the pill: a more obvious candidate, this, for a Wodehousian hero of the Restoration — a helpless, self-opinionated innocent whom we simply cannot help liking. He, clearly, is far happier amongst the drones than amongst all those threatening females. Yet so too, on the evidence of that laidback first act, in which the only woman present is a compliant lower-class bawd, is Dorimant — a Bertie Wooster blessed and cursed with being his own Jeeves.

For Further Reading

Until relatively recently, far less critical interest has been shown in Etherege than in the other major 'Restoration' dramatists, and he was not even included in the otherwise wide-ranging Mermaid Series in the late nineteenth century. An inadequate edition by A.W. Verity did appear in 1888, but the standard modern edition was prepared by H.F.B. Brett-Smith — the two-volume *Dramatic Works* (Oxford: Blackwell, 1927; reprinted, St. Clair Shores, Mich.: Scholarly Press, 1971), and there is also now a convenient single-volume edition by Michael Cordner (Cambridge University Press, 1982), which has the rare virtue of preserving Etherege's theatrical (rather than grammatical) punctuation. There are also individual critical editions of *The Man of Mode* by W.B Carnochan for the Regents Restoration Drama Series (London: Arnold, 1967), by John Conaghan for the Fountainwell Drama Texts (Edinburgh: Oliver and Boyd, 1973), and by John Barnard for the New Mermaid Series (London:

Benn, 1979). *The Letters of Sir George Etherege* have been most recently edited by Frederick Bracher (Berkeley: University of California Press, 1974).

The best of the full-length studies of Etherege, though its viewpoint is entirely literary critical, remains Dale Underwood's *Etherege and the Seventeenth-Century Comedy of Manners* (Yale University Press, 1957), which is far superior to an earlier work by F.S. McCamic, *Etherege: a Study in Restoration Comedy* (Cedar Rapids, Iowa, 1931). *The Man of Mode* has, however, received a more generous share of attention in the journals — again, mainly from a literary-critical standpoint, though an exception, despite the unlikely title, is Edward A. Langhans's 'An Edinburgh Promptbook from 1679-80', in *Theatre Notebook*, XXXVII (1983). Other recent studies include a response to Underwood by John Hayman, 'Poise is Not Equivocation', in *Essays in Criticism,* X (1960); a valuable piece by Jocelyn Powell, 'George Etherege and the Form of Comedy', in *Restoration Theatre,* edited by John Russell Brown and Bernard Harris (London: Arnold, 1965); two contrasting views of the play's ethical standpoint, John Traugott's 'The Rake's Progress from Court to Comedy', in *Studies in English Literature,* VI (1966), and David Krause's 'The Defaced Angel: a Concept of Satanic Grace in Etherege's *The Man of Mode*', in *Drama Survey,* VII (1968-69); Paul C. Davies's 'The State of Nature and the State of War', in *University of Toronto Quarterly,* XXXIX (1969); a useful study of the 'etiquette' of the play by John Hayman, 'Dorimant and the Comedy of a Man of Mode', in *Modern Language Quarterly,* XXX (1969); Ronald Berman's 'The Comic Passions of *The Man of Mode*', in *Studies in English Literature,* X (1970); and two useful analyses of critical disagreements over the play, Robert D. Hume's 'Reading and Misreading *The Man of Mode*', in *Criticism,* XIV (1972), and Brian Corman's 'Interpreting and Misinterpreting *The Man of Mode*', in *Papers on Language and Literature,* XII (1977).

Of three recent books on the theatrical style and conventions of the period, Peter Holland's *The Ornament of Action: Text and Performance in Restoration Comedy* (Cambridge University Press, 1979), is particularly helpful on Etherege, but Jocelyn Powell's *Restoration Theatre Production* (London: Routledge, 1984) and J.L. Styan's *Restoration Comedy in Performance* (Cambridge University Press, 1986) remain valuable and are often complementary. Recommended among general studies of the drama and theatre are R.D. Hume's *The Development of English Drama in the Late Seventeenth Century* (Clarendon Press, 1976) and *The London Stage 1660-1700: a Critical Introduction* (Southern Illinois University Press, 1968).

THE PROGRAMME

In addition to cast list, biographies and play notes,
the programme you have purchased for this
performance contains the full text of the play.
Please would you bear in mind that following the
text during the performance is very distracting to
the performers especially when you are seated
in rows close to the stage.

Thank you for your help.

The Text

The text used and reproduced here is taken from the edition edited
by John Barnard for the New Mermaids Series (Ernest Benn Ltd,
1979). In that edition Etherege's own stage directions were
retained but were amplified, although minimally. All editorial
additions are given between braces. The cuts made in the RSC
version are indicated by square brackets in the text.

THE MAN OF MODE

by George Etherege

(Sir Fopling Flutter)

To Her Royal Highness the Duchess

MADAM, Poets, however they may be modest otherwise, have always too good an opinion of what they write. The world, when it sees this play dedicated to your Royal Highness, will conclude I have more than my share of that vanity. But I hope the honour I have of belonging to you will excuse my presumption. 'Tis the first thing I have produced in your service, and my duty obliges me to what my choice durst not else have aspired.

I am very sensible, Madam, how much it is beholding to your indulgence for the success it had in the acting, and your protection will be no less fortunate to it in the printing; for all are so ambitious of making their court to you, that none can be severe to what you are pleased to favour.

This universal submission and respect is due to the greatness of your rank and birth; but you have other illustrious qualities which are much more engaging. Those would but dazzle, did not these really charm the eyes and understandings of all who have the happiness to approach you.

Authors on these occasions are never wanting to publish a particular of their patron's virtues and perfections; but your Royal Highness's are so eminently known that, did I follow their examples, I should but paint those wonders here of which every-one already has the idea in his mind. Besides, I do not think it proper to aim at that in prose which is so glorious a subject for verse, in which hereafter if I show more zeal than skill, it will not grieve me much, since I less passionately desire to be esteemed a poet than to be thought,

Madam,
Your Royal Highness's
most humble, most obedient,
and most faithful servant,
GEORGE ETHEREGE

Dramatis Personae

GENTLEMEN

MR DORIMANT
MR MEDLEY, *his friend*
OLD BELLAIR
YOUNG BELLAIR, *his son, in love with Emilia*
SIR FOPLING FLUTTER

GENTLEWOMEN

LADY TOWNLEY, *sister of Old Bellair*
EMILIA
MRS LOVEIT, *in love with Dorimant*
BELLINDA, *in love with Dorimant*
LADY WOODVILL
HARRIET, *her daughter*

WAITING WOMEN

PERT
BUSY

A SHOEMAKER
AN ORANGE-WOMAN
FOUR SLOVENLY BULLIES
TWO CHAIRMEN
MR SMIRK, *a parson*
HANDY, *a valet de chambre*
PAGES, FOOTMEN, *etc.*

Prologue

BY SIR CAR SCROOPE, BARONET

Like dancers on the ropes poor poets fare:
Most perish young, the rest in danger are.
This, one would think, should make our authors wary,
But, gamester-like, the giddy fools miscarry;
A lucky hand or two so tempts 'em on,
They cannot leave off play till they're undone.
With modest fears a Muse does first begin,
Like a young wench newly enticed to sin;
But tickled once with praise, by her good will,
The wanton fool would never more lie still.
'Tis an old mistress you'll meet here tonight,
Whose charms you once looked on with delight.
But now, of late, such dirty drabs have known ye,
A muse o'the better sort's ashamed to own ye.
Nature well-drawn and wit must now give place
To gaudy nonsense and to dull grimace;
Nor is it strange that you should like so much
That kind of wit, for most of yours is such.
But I'm afraid that while to France we go,
To bring you home fine dresses, dance, and show,
The stage, like you, will but more foppish grow.
Of foreign wares why should we fetch the scum,
When we can be so richly served at home?
For, heav'n be thanked, 'tis not so wise an age
But your own follies may supply the stage.
Though often ploughed, there's no great fear the soil
Should barren grow by the too-frequent toil,
While at your doors are to be daily found
Such loads of dunghill to manure the ground.
'Tis by your follies that we players thrive,
As the physicians by diseases live;
And as each new year some new distemper reigns,
Whose friendly poison helps t'increase their gains,
So, among you, there starts up every day
Some new, unheard-of fool for us to play.
Then, for your own sakes, be not too severe,
Nor what you all admire at home, damn here.
Since each is fond of his own ugly face,
Why should you, when we hold it, break the glass?

ACT ONE

A dressing room. A table covered with a toilet; clothes laid ready.

Enter Dorimant in his gown and slippers, with a note in his hand made up, repeating verses.

DORIMANT.
'Now, for some ages, had the pride of Spain
Made the sun shine on half the world in vain'.

Then looking on the note

'For Mrs Loveit'. What a dull, insipid thing is a billet doux written in cold blood after the heat of the business is over! It is a tax upon good nature which I have here been labouring to pay, and have done it, but with as much regret as ever fanatic paid the Royal Aid or church duties. 'Twill have the same fate, I know, that all my notes to her have had of late – 'twill not be thought kind enough. Faith, women are i' the right when they jealously examine our letters, for in them we always first discover our decay of passion. – Hey! Who waits?

Enter Handy

HANDY.
Sir –

DORIMANT.
Call a footman.

HANDY.
None of 'em are come yet.

DORIMANT.
Dogs! Will they ever lie snoring abed till noon?

HANDY.
'Tis all one, sir: if they're up, you indulge 'em so, they're ever poaching after whores all the morning.

DORIMANT.
Take notice henceforward who's wanting in his duty – the next clap he gets, he shall rot for an example. What vermin are those chattering without?

HANDY.
Foggy Nan, the orange-woman, and swearing Tom, the shoemaker.

DORIMANT.
Go, call in that overgrown jade with the flasket of guts before

her. Fruit is refreshing in a morning.

Exit Handy

'It is not that I love you less,
Than when before your feet I lay –'

Enter Orange-Woman {and Handy}

How now, double-tripe, what news do you bring?

ORANGE-WOMAN.
News! Here's the best fruit has come to town t'year. Gad, I was up before four o'clock this morning and bought all the choice i' the market.

DORIMANT.
The nasty refuse of your shop.

ORANGE-WOMAN.
You need not make mouths at it. I assure you, 'tis all culled ware.

DORIMANT.
The citizens buy better on a holiday in their walk to Tot'nam.

ORANGE-WOMAN.
Good or bad, 'tis all one; I never knew you commend anything. Lord, would the ladies had heard you talk of 'em as I have done. Here –

Sets down the fruit

Bid your man give me an angel.

DORIMANT *{to Handy}*
Give the bawd her fruit again.

ORANGE-WOMAN.
Well, on my conscience, there never was the like of you – God's my life, I had almost forgot to tell you, there is a young gentlewoman, lately come to town with her mother, that is so taken with you.

DORIMANT.
Is she handsome?

ORANGE-WOMAN.
Nay, gad, there are few finer women, I tell you but so, and a hugeous fortune, they say. Here, eat this peach, it comes from the stone. 'Tis better than any Newington you've tasted.

DORIMANT.
This fine woman, I'll lay my life (*taking the peach*), is some awkward, ill-fashioned country toad, who, not having above four dozen of black hairs on her head, has adorned her baldness with a large white fruz, that she may look sparkishly in the forefront of the King's box at an old play.

ORANGE-WOMAN.
Gad, you'd change your note quickly if you did but see her!

DORIMANT.
How came she to know me?

ORANGE-WOMAN.
She saw you yesterday at the Change. She told me you came and fooled with the woman at the next shop.

DORIMANT.
I remember, there was a mask observed me, indeed. Fooled, did she say?

ORANGE-WOMAN.
Ay; I vow she told me twenty things you said too, and acted with her head and with her body so like you –

Enter Medley

MEDLEY.
Dorimant, my life, my joy, my darling sin! How dost thou? {*Embraces him*}

ORANGE-WOMAN.
Lord, what a filthy trick these men have got of kissing one another! *She spits.*

MEDLEY.
Why do you suffer this cartload of scandal to come near you and make your neighbours think you so improvident to need a bawd?

ORANGE-WOMAN *{to Dorimant}*
Good, now we shall have it! You did but want him to help you. Come, pay me for my fruit.

MEDLEY.
Make us thankful for it, huswife. Bawds are as much out of fashion as gentlemen-ushers: none but old formal ladies use the one, and none but foppish old stagers employ the other. Go, you are an insignificant brandy bottle.

DORIMANT.
Nay, there you wrong her. Three quarts of canary is her business.

ORANGE-WOMAN.
What you please, gentlemen.

DORIMANT.
To him! Give him as good as he brings.

ORANGE-WOMAN.
Hang him, there is not such another heathen in the town again, except it be the shoemaker without.

MEDLEY.
I shall see you hold up your hand at the bar next sessions for murder, huswife. That shoemaker can take his oath you are in fee with the doctors to sell green fruit to the gentry, that the crudities may breed diseases.

ORANGE-WOMAN.
Pray give me my money.

DORIMANT.
Not a penny! When you bring the gentlewoman hither you spoke of, you shall be paid.

ORANGE-WOMAN.
The gentlewoman! The gentlewoman may be as honest as your sisters, for aught as I know. Pray pay me, Mr Dorimant, and do not abuse me so. I have an honester way of living – you know it.

MEDLEY.
Was there ever such a resty bawd?

DORIMANT.
Some jade's trick she has, but she makes amends when she's in good humour. Come, tell me the lady's name, and Handy shall pay you.

ORANGE-WOMAN.
I must not, she forbid me.

DORIMANT.
That's a sure sign she would have you.

MEDLEY.
Where does she live?

ORANGE-WOMAN.
They lodge at my house.

MEDLEY.
Nay, then she's in a hopeful way.

ORANGE-WOMAN.
Good Mr Medley, say your pleasure of me, but take heed how you affront my house. God's my life, in a hopeful way!

DORIMANT.
Prithee, peace. What kind of woman's the mother?

ORANGE-WOMAN.
A goodly, grave gentlewoman. Lord, how she talks against the wild young men o' the town! As for your part, she thinks you an arrant devil: should she see you, on my conscience she would look if you had not a cloven foot.

DORIMANT.
Does she know me?

ORANGE-WOMAN.
Only by hearsay. A thousand horrid stories have been told her of you, and she believes 'em all.

MEDLEY.
By the character, this should be the famous Lady Woodvill and her daughter Harriet.

ORANGE-WOMAN {*aside*}
The devil's in him for guessing, I think.

DORIMANT.
Do you know 'em?

MEDLEY.
Both very well. The mother's a great admirer of the forms and civility of the last age.

DORIMANT.
An antiquated beauty may be allowed to be out of humour at the freedoms of the present. This is a good account of the mother. Pray, what is the daughter?

MEDLEY.
Why, first, she's an heiress, vastly rich.

DORIMANT.
And handsome?

MEDLEY.
What alteration a twelvemonth may have bred in her, I know not, but a year ago she was the beautifullest creature I ever saw – a fine, easy, clean shape, light brown hair in abundance, her features regular, her complexion clear, and lively, large, wanton eyes; but, above all, a mouth that has made me kiss it a thousand times in imagination – teeth white and even, and pretty, pouting lips, with a little moisture ever hanging on them, that look like the Provence rose fresh on the bush, ere the morning sun has quite drawn up the dew.

DORIMANT.
Rapture, mere rapture!

ORANGE-WOMAN.
Nay, gad, he tells you true. She's a delicate creature.

DORIMANT.
Has she wit?

MEDLEY.

More than is usual in her sex, and as much malice. Then, she's as wild as you would wish her, and has a demureness in her looks that makes it so surprising.

DORIMANT.

Flesh and blood cannot hear this and not long to know her.

MEDLEY.

I wonder what makes her mother bring her up to town? An old, doting keeper cannot be more jealous of his mistress.

ORANGE-WOMAN.

She made me laugh yesterday. There was a judge came to visit 'em, and the old man (she told me) did so stare upon her and, when he saluted her, smacked so heartily – who would think it of 'em?

MEDLEY.

God-a-mercy, Judge!

DORIMANT.

Do 'em right, the gentlemen of the long robe have not been wanting by their good examples to countenance the crying sin o' the nation.

MEDLEY.

Come, on with your trappings; 'tis later than you imagine.

DORIMANT.

Call in the shoemaker, Handy!

ORANGE-WOMAN.

Good Mr Dorimant, pay me. Gad, I had rather give you my fruit than stay to be abused by that foul-mouthed rogue. What you gentlemen say, it matters not much, but such a dirty fellow does one more disgrace.

DORIMANT {to Handy}

Give her ten shillings. {to Orange-Woman} And be sure you tell the young gentlewoman I must be acquainted with her.

ORANGE-WOMAN.

Now do you long to be tempting this pretty creature. Well, heavens mend you!

MEDLEY.

Farewell, bog!

Exeunt Orange-Woman and Handy

Dorimant, when did you see your *pis aller*, as you call her, Mrs Loveit?

DORIMANT.

Not these two days.

MEDLEY.

And how 'stand affairs between you?

DORIMANT.

There has been great patching of late, much ado – we make a shift to hang together.

MEDLEY.

I wonder how her mighty spirit bears it?

DORIMANT.

Ill enough, on all conscience. I never knew so violent a creature.

MEDLEY.

She's the most passionate in her love and the most extravagant in her jealousy of any woman I ever heard of. What note is that?

DORIMANT.

An excuse I am going to send her for the neglect I am guilty of.

MEDLEY.

Prithee, read it.

DORIMANT.

No, but if you will take the pains, you may.

MEDLEY (*reads*)

'I never was a lover of business, but now I have a just reason to hate it, since it has kept me these two days from seeing you. I intend to wait upon you in the afternoon, and in the pleasure of your conversation forget all I have suffered during this tedious absence'. – This business of yours, Dorimant, has been with a vizard at the playhouse; I have had an eye on you. If some malicious body should betray you, this kind note would hardly make your peace with her.

DORIMANT.

I desire no better.

MEDLEY.

Why, would her knowledge of it oblige you?

DORIMANT.

Most infinitely; next to the coming to a good understanding with a new mistress, I love a quarrel with an old one. But the devil's in't, there has been such a calm in my affairs of late, I have not had the pleasure of making a woman so much as break her fan, to be sullen, or forswear herself, these three days.

MEDLEY.

A very great misfortune! Let me see, I love mischief well

enough to forward this business myself. I'll about it presently, and though I know the truth of what you've done, will set her a-raving. I'll heighten it a little with invention, leave her in a fit o' the mother, and be here again before you're ready.

DORIMANT.
Pray, stay; you may spare yourself the labour. The business is undertaken already by one who will manage it with as much address and, I think, with a little more malice than you can.

MEDLEY.
Who i' the devil's name can this be?

DORIMANT.
Why, the vizard, that very vizard you saw me with.

MEDLEY.
Does she love mischief so well as to betray herself to spite another?

DORIMANT.
Not so neither, Medley; I will make you comprehend the mystery. This mask, for a farther confirmation of what I have been these two days swearing to her, made me yesterday at the playhouse make her a promise, before her face, utterly to break off with Loveit; and because she tenders my reputation and would not have me do a barbarous thing, has contrived a way to give me a handsome occasion.

MEDLEY.
Very good.

DORIMANT.
She intends, about an hour before me this afternoon, to make Loveit a visit; and having the privilege, by reason of a professed friendship between 'em, to talk of her concerns –

MEDLEY.
Is she a friend?

DORIMANT.
Oh, an intimate friend!

MEDLEY.
Better and better! Pray proceed.

DORIMANT.
She means insensibly to insinuate a discourse of me, and artificially raise her jealousy to such a height that, transported with the first motions of her passion, she shall fly upon me with all the fury imaginable as soon as ever I enter. The quarrel being thus happily begun, I am to play my part: confess and justify all my roguery, swear her impertinence

and ill humour makes her intolerable, tax her with the next fop that comes into my head, and in a huff march away, slight her, and leave her to be taken by whosoever thinks it worth his time to lie down before her.

MEDLEY.
This vizard is a spark, and has a genius that makes her worthy of yourself, Dorimant.

Enter Handy, Shoemaker, and Footman

DORIMANT {*to Footman*}
You rogue there, who sneak like a dog that has flung down a dish, if you do not mend your waiting, I'll uncase you and turn you loose to the wheel of fortune. – Handy, seal this and let him run with it presently.

Exeunt Handy and Footman

{*Handy re-enters after a few moments*}

MEDLEY.
Since you're resolved on a quarrel, why do you send her this kind note?

DORIMANT.
To keep her at home in order to the business. (*To the Shoemaker*) How now, you drunken sot?

SHOEMAKER.
'Zbud, you have no reason to talk. I have not had a bottle of sack of yours in my belly this fortnight.

MEDLEY.
The orange-woman says your neighbours take notice what a heathen you are, and design to inform the bishop and have you burned for an atheist.

SHOEMAKER.
Damn her, dunghill! If her husband does not remove her, she stinks so, the parish intend to indict him for a nuisance.

MEDLEY.
I advise you like a friend, reform your life. You have brought the envy of the world upon you by living above yourself. Whoring and swearing are vices too genteel for a shoemaker.

SHOEMAKER.
'Zbud, I think you men of quality will grow as unreasonable as the women: you would engross the sins o' the nation. Poor folks can no sooner be wicked but they're railed at by their betters.

DORIMANT.
Sirrah, I'll have you stand i' the pillory for this libel.

SHOEMAKER.

Some of you deserve it, I'm sure. There are so many of 'em that our journeymen nowadays, instead of harmless ballads, sing nothing but your damned lampoons.

DORIMANT.

Our lampoons, you rogue?

SHOEMAKER.

Nay, good master, why should not you write your own commentaries as well as Caesar?

MEDLEY.

The rascal's read, I perceive.

SHOEMAKER.

You know the old proverb – ale and history.

DORIMANT.

Draw on my shoes, sirrah.

SHOEMAKER.

Here's a shoe –

DORIMANT.

Sits with more wrinkles than there are in an angry bully's forehead.

SHOEMAKER.

'Zbud, as smooth as your mistress's skin does upon her. So, strike your foot in home. 'Zbud, if e'er a monsieur of 'em all make more fashionable ware, I'll be content to have my ears whipped off with my own paring knife.

MEDLEY.

And served up in a ragout, instead of cockcombs, to a company of French shoemakers for a collation.

SHOEMAKER.

Hold, hold! Damn 'em caterpillars! Let 'em feed upon cabbage! – Come master, your health this morning! – next my heart now!

DORIMANT.

Go, get you home, and govern your family better! Do not let your wife follow you to the alehouse, beat your whore, and lead you home in triumph.

SHOEMAKER.

'Zbud, there's never a man i' the town lives more like a gentleman with his wife than I do. I never mind her motions; she never inquires into mine. We speak to one another civilly, hate one another heartily, and because 'tis vulgar to lie and soak together, we have each of us our several settle-bed.

DORIMANT {to Handy}

Give him half a crown.

MEDLEY.

Not without he will promise to be bloody drunk.

SHOEMAKER.

Tope's the word, i' the eye of the world. {To Handy} For my master's honour, Robin!

DORIMANT.

Do not debauch my servants, sirrah.

SHOEMAKER.

I only tip him the wink; he knows an alehouse from a hovel.

Exit Shoemaker

DORIMANT {to Handy}

My clothes, quickly!

MEDLEY.

Where shall we dine today?

Enter Young Bellair

DORIMANT.

Where you will. Here comes a good third man.

YOUNG BELLAIR.

Your servant, gentlemen.

MEDLEY.

Gentle sir, how will you answer this visit to your honourable mistress? 'Tis not her interest you should keep company with men of sense, who will be talking reason.

YOUNG BELLAIR.

I do not fear her pardon, do you but grant me yours for my neglect of late.

MEDLEY.

Though you've made us miserable by the want of your good company, to show you I am free from all resentment, may the beautiful cause of our misfortune give you all the joys happy lovers have shared ever since the world began.

YOUNG BELLAIR.

You wish me in heaven, but you believe me on my journey to hell.

MEDLEY.

You have a good strong faith, and that may contribute much towards your salvation. I confess I am but of an untoward constitution, apt to have doubts and scruples; and in love they are no less distracting than in religion. Were I so near marriage, I should cry out by fits as I ride in my coach, 'Cuckold, cuckold!' with no less fury than the mad fanatic does 'Glory!' in Bethlem.

YOUNG BELLAIR.
Because religion makes some run mad, must I live an atheist?

MEDLEY.
Is it not great indiscretion for a man of credit, who may have money enough on his word, to go and deal with Jews, who for little sums make men enter into bonds and give judgments?

YOUNG BELLAIR.
Preach no more on this text. I am determined, and there is no hope of my conversion.

DORIMANT (*to Handy, who is fiddling about him*)
Leave your unnecessary fiddling. A wasp that's buzzing about a man's nose at dinner is not more troublesome than thou art.

HANDY.
You love to have your clothes hang just, sir.

DORIMANT.
I love to be well-dressed, sir, and think it no scandal to my understanding.

HANDY.
Will you use the essence, or orange-flower water?

DORIMANT.
I will smell as I do today, no offence to the ladies' noses.

HANDY.
Your pleasure, sir.

{*Exit Handy*}

DORIMANT.
That a man's excellency should lie in neatly tying of a ribbon or a cravat! How careful's nature in furnishing the world with necessary coxcombs!

YOUNG BELLAIR.
That's a mighty pretty suit of yours, Dorimant.

DORIMANT.
I am glad 't has your approbation.

YOUNG BELLAIR.
No man in town has a better fancy in his clothes than you have.

DORIMANT.
You will make me have an opinion of my genius.

MEDLEY.
There is a great critic, I hear, in these matters lately arrived piping hot from Paris.

YOUNG BELLAIR.
Sir Fopling Flutter, you mean.

MEDLEY.
The same.

YOUNG BELLAIR.
He thinks himself the pattern of modern gallantry.

DORIMANT.
He is indeed the pattern of modern foppery.

MEDLEY.
He was yesterday at the play, with a pair of gloves up to his elbows and a periwig more exactly curled than a lady's head newly dressed for a ball.

YOUNG BELLAIR.
What a pretty lisp he has!

DORIMANT.
Ho, that he affects in imitation of the people of quality of France.

MEDLEY.
His head stands for the most part on one side, and his looks are more languishing than a lady's when she lolls at stretch in her coach or leans her head carelessly against the side of a box i' the playhouse.

DORIMANT.
He is a person indeed of great acquired follies.

MEDLEY.
He is like many others, beholding to his education for making him so eminent a coxcomb. Many a fool had been lost to the world, had their indulgent parents wisely bestowed neither learning nor good breeding on 'em.

YOUNG BELLAIR.
He has been, as the sparkish word is, brisk upon the ladies already. He was yesterday at my Aunt Townley's and gave Mrs Loveit a catalogue of his good qualities under the character of a complete gentleman, who (according to Sir Fopling) ought to dress well, dance well, fence well, have a genius for love letters, an agreeable voice for a chamber, be very amorous, something discreet, but not over-constant.

MEDLEY.
Pretty ingredients to make an accomplished person!

DORIMANT.
I am glad he pitched upon Loveit.

YOUNG BELLAIR.
How so?

DORIMANT.
I wanted a fop to lay to her charge, and this is as pat as may be.

YOUNG BELLAIR.
I am confident she loves no man but you.

DORIMANT.
The good fortune were enough to make me vain, but that I am in my nature modest.

YOUNG BELLAIR.
Hark you, Dorimant. – With your leave, Mr Medley – 'tis only a secret concerning a fair lady.

MEDLEY.
Your good breeding, sir, gives you too much trouble. You might have whispered without all this ceremony.

YOUNG BELLAIR (*to Dorimant*)
How stand your affairs with Bellinda of late?

DORIMANT.
She's a little jilting baggage.

YOUNG BELLAIR.
Nay, I believe her false enough, but she's ne'er the worse for your purpose. She was with you yesterday in a disguise at the play.

DORIMANT.
There we fell out and resolved never to speak to one another more.

YOUNG BELLAIR.
The occasion?

DORIMANT.
Want of courage to meet me at the place appointed. These young women apprehend loving as much as the young men do fighting at first; but once entered, like them too, they all turn bullies straight.

Enter Handy

HANDY (*to Young Bellair*)
Sir, your man without desires to speak with you.

YOUNG BELLAIR.
Gentlemen, I'll return immediately.

Exit Young Bellair

MEDLEY.
A very pretty fellow, this.

DORIMANT.
He's handsome, well-bred, and by much the most tolerable of all the young men that do not abound in wit.

MEDLEY.
Ever well-dressed, always complaisant, and seldom impertinent. You and he are grown very intimate, I see.

DORIMANT.
It is our mutual interest to be so. It makes the women think the better of his understanding and judge more favourably of my reputation; it makes him pass upon some for a man of very good sense, and I upon others for a very civil person.

MEDLEY.
What was that whisper?

DORIMANT.
A thing which he would fain have known, but I did not think it fit to tell him. It might have frighted him from his honourable intentions of marrying.

MEDLEY.
Emilia, give her her due, has the best reputation of any young woman about the town who has beauty enough to provoke detraction. Her carriage is unaffected, her discourse modest – not at all censorious not pretending, like the counterfeits of the age.

DORIMANT.
She's a discreet maid, and I believe nothing can corrupt her but a husband.

MEDLEY.
A husband?

DORIMANT.
Yes, a husband. I have known many women make a difficulty of losing a maidenhead, who have afterwards made none of making a cuckold.

MEDLEY.
This prudent consideration, I am apt to think, has made you confirm poor Bellair in the desperate resolution he has taken.

DORIMANT.
Indeed, the little hope I found there was of her, in the state she was in, has made me by my advice contribute something towards the changing of her condition.

Enter Young Bellair

Dear Bellair, by heavens I thought we had lost thee! Men in love are never to be reckoned on when we would form a company.

YOUNG BELLAIR.
Dorimant, I am undone. My man has brought the most surprising news i' the world.

DORIMANT.
Some strange misfortune is befallen your love?

YOUNG BELLAIR.
My father came to town last night and lodges i' the very house where Emilia lies.

MEDLEY.
Does he know it is with her you are in love?

YOUNG BELLAIR.
He knows I love, but knows not whom, without some officious sot has betrayed me.

DORIMANT.
Your Aunt Townley is your confidante and favours the business.

YOUNG BELLAIR.
I do not apprehend any ill office from her. I have received a letter, in which I am commanded by my father to meet him at my aunt's this afternoon. He tells me farther he has made a match for me, and bids me resolve to be obedient to his will or expect to be disinherited.

MEDLEY.
Now's your time, Bellair. Never had lover such an opportunity of giving a generous proof of his passion.

YOUNG BELLAIR.
As how, I pray?

MEDLEY.
Why, hang an estate, marry Emilia out of hand, and provoke your father to do what he threatens. 'Tis but despising a coach, humbling yourself to a pair of galoshes, being out of countenance when you meet your friends, pointed at and pitied wherever you go by all the amorous fops that know you, and your fame will be immortal.

YOUNG BELLAIR.
I could find in my heart to resolve not to marry at all.

DORIMANT.
Fie, fie! That would spoil a good jest and disappoint the well-natured town of an occasion of laughing at you.

YOUNG BELLAIR.
The storm I have so long expected hangs o'er my head and begins to pour down upon me. I am on the rack and can have no rest till I'm satisfied in what I fear. Where do you dine?

DORIMANT.
At Long's or Locket's.

MEDLEY.
At Long's let it be.

YOUNG BELLAIR.
I'll run and see Emilia and inform myself how matters stand. If my misfortunes are not so great as to make me unfit for company, I'll be with you.

Exit Young Bellair

Enter a Footman with a letter

FOOTMAN (*to Dorimant*)
Here's a letter, sir.

DORIMANT.
The superscription's right: 'For Mr Dorimant'.

MEDLEY.
Let's see. (*Looks at the letter*) The very scrawl and spelling of a true-bred whore.

DORIMANT.
I know the hand. The style is admirable, I assure you.

MEDLEY.
Prithee, read it.

DORIMANT (*reads*).
'I told a you you dud not love me, if you dud, you would have seen me again ere now. I have no money and am very malicolly. Pray send me a guynie to see the operies. Your servant to command, Molly'.

MEDLEY.
Pray let the whore have a favourable answer, that she may spark it in a box and do honour to her profession.

DORIMANT.
She shall, and perk up i' the face of quality. {*To Handy*} Is the coach at door?

HANDY.
You did not bid me send for it.

DORIMANT.
Eternal blockhead! (*Handy offers to go out*) Hey, sot!

HANDY.
   Did you call me, sir?

DORIMANT.
   I hope you have no just exception to the name, sir?

HANDY.
   I have sense, sir.

DORIMANT.
   Not so much as a fly in winter. – How did you come, Medley?

MEDLEY.
   In a chair.

FOOTMAN.
   You may have a hackney coach if you please, sir.

DORIMANT.
   I may ride the elephant if I please, sir. Call another chair and let my coach follow to Long's.
         'Be calm, ye great parents, etc.'

                              Exeunt, {Dorimant} singing

ACT TWO

Scene One

{Lady Townley's house}
Enter my Lady Townley and Emilia

LADY TOWNLEY.
   I was afraid, Emilia, all had been discovered.

EMILIA.
   I tremble with the apprehension still.

LADY TOWNLEY.
   That my brother should take lodgings i' the very house where you lie!

EMILIA.
   'Twas lucky we had timely notice to warn the people to be secret. He seems to be a mighty good-humoured old man.

LADY TOWNLEY.
   He ever had a notable smirking way with him.

EMILIA.
   He calls me rogue, tells me he can't abide me, and does so bepat me.

LADY TOWNLEY.
   On my word, you are much in his favour then.

EMILIA.
   He has been very inquisitive, I am told, about my family, my reputation, and my fortune.

LADY TOWNLEY.
   I am confident he does not i' the least suspect you are the woman his son's in love with.

EMILIA.
   What should make him then inform himself so particularly of me?

LADY TOWNLEY.
   He was always of a very loving temper himself. It may be he has a doting fit upon him, who knows?

EMILIA.
   It cannot be.

Enter Young Bellair

LADY TOWNLEY.
   Here comes my nephew. – Where did you leave your father?

YOUNG BELLAIR.

Writing a note within. Emilia, this early visit looks as if some kind jealousy would not let you rest at home.

EMILIA.

The knowledge I have of my rival gives me a little cause to fear your constancy.

YOUNG BELLAIR. My constancy! I vow –

EMILIA.

Do not vow – our love is frail as is our life, and full as little in our power; and are you sure you shall outlive this day?

YOUNG BELLAIR.

I am not, but when we are in perfect health, 'twere an idle thing to fright ourselves with the thoughts of sudden death.

LADY TOWNLEY.

Pray, what has passed between you and your father i' the garden?

YOUNG BELLAIR.

He's firm in his resolution, tells me I must marry Mrs Harriet, or swears he'll marry himself and disinherit me. When I saw I could not prevail with him to be more indulgent, I dissembled an obedience to his will, which has composed his passion and will give us time – and I hope opportunity – to deceive him.

Enter Old Bellair with a note in his hand

LADY TOWNLEY.

Peace, here he comes.

OLD BELLAIR.

Harry, take this and let your man carry it for me to Mr Fourbe's chamber, my lawyer, i' the Temple.

{*Exit Young Bellair*}

(*To Emilia*) Neighbour, adod, I am glad to see thee here. – Make much of her, sister. She's one of the best of your acquaintance. I like her countenance and her behaviour well; she has a modesty that is not common i' this age, adod she has.

LADY TOWNLEY.

I know her value, brother, and esteem her accordingly.

OLD BELLAIR.

Advise her to wear a little more mirth in her face. Adod, she's too serious.

LADY TOWNLEY.

The fault is very excusable in a young woman.

OLD BELLAIR.

Nay, adod, I like ne'er the worse; a melancholy beauty has her charms. I love a pretty sadness in a face which varies now and then, like changeable colours, into a smile.

LADY TOWNLEY.

Methinks you speak very feelingly, brother.

OLD BELLAIR.

I am but five-and-fifty, sister, you know – an age not altogether insensible. (*To Emilia*) Cheer up sweetheart, I have a secret to tell thee may chance to make thee merry. We three will make collation together anon. I' the meantime, mum! {*Aloud*} I can't abide you; go, I can't abide you –

Enter Young Bellair

Harry! Come, you must along with me to my Lady Woodvill's. – I am going to slip the boy at a mistress.

YOUNG BELLAIR.

At a wife, sir, you would say.

OLD BELLAIR.

You need not look so glum, sir. A wife is no curse when she brings the blessing of a good estate with her. But an idle town flirt, with a painted face, a rotten reputation, and a crazy fortune, adod, is the devil and all; and such a one I hear you are in league with.

YOUNG BELLAIR.

I cannot help detraction, sir.

OLD BELLAIR.

Out a pize o' their breeches, there are keeping fools enough for such flaunting baggages, and they are e'en too good for 'em. (*To Emilia*) Remember 'night {*Aloud*} Go, you're a rogue, you're a rogue. Fare you well, fare you well. {*To Young Bellair*} Come, come, come along, sir.

Exeunt Old and Young Bellair

LADY TOWNLEY.

On my word, the old man comes on apace. I'll lay my life he's smitten.

EMILIA.

This is nothing but the pleasantness of his humour.

LADY TOWNLEY.

I know him better than you. Let it work; it may prove lucky.

Enter a Page

PAGE.
Madam, Mr Medley has sent to know whether a visit will not be troublesome this afternoon?

LADY TOWNLEY.
Send him word his visits never are so.

{*Exit Page*}

EMILIA.
He's a very pleasant man.

LADY TOWNLEY.
He's a very necessary man among us women. He's not scandalous i' the least, perpetually contriving to bring good company together, and always ready to stop up a gap at ombre. Then, he knows all the little news o' the town.

EMILIA.
I love to hear him talk o' the intrigues. Let 'em be never so dull in themselves, he'll make 'em pleasant i' the relation.

LADY TOWNLEY.
But he improves things so much one can take no measure of the truth from him. Mr Dorimant swears a flea or a maggot is not made more monstrous by a magnifying glass than a story is by his telling it.

Enter Medley

EMILIA.
Hold, here he comes.

LADY TOWNLEY.
Mr Medley.

MEDLEY.
Your servant, madam.

LADY TOWNLEY.
You have made yourself a stranger of late.

EMILIA.
I believe you took a surfeit of ombre last time you were here.

MEDLEY.
Indeed I had my bellyful of that termagant, Lady Dealer. There never was so insatiable a carder; an old gleeker never loved to sit to 't like her. I have played with her now at least a dozen times, till she's worn out all her fine complexion and her tour would keep in curl no longer.

LADY TOWNLEY.
Blame her not, poor woman. She loves nothing so well as a black ace.

MEDLEY.
The pleasure I have seen her in when she has had hope in drawing for a matadore!

EMILIA.
'Tis as pretty sport to her as persuading masks off is to you, to make discoveries.

LADY TOWNLEY.
Pray, where's your friend Mr Dorimant?

MEDLEY.
Soliciting his affairs. He's a man of great employment – has more mistresses now depending than the most eminent lawyer in England has causes.

EMILIA.
Here has been Mrs Loveit so uneasy and out of humour these two days.

LADY TOWNLEY.
How strangely love and jealousy rage in that poor woman!

MEDLEY.
She could not have picked out a devil upon earth so proper to torment her. He's made her break a dozen or two of fans already, tear half a score points in pieces, and destroy hoods and knots without number.

LADY TOWNLEY.
We heard of a pleasant serenade he gave her t'other night.

MEDLEY.
A Danish serenade, with kettledrums and trumpets.

EMILIA.
Oh, barbarous!

MEDLEY.
What, you are of the number of the ladies whose ears are grown so delicate since our operas, you can be charmed with nothing but flutes douces and French hautboys?

EMILIA.
Leave your raillery and tell us, is there any new wit come forth – songs, or novels?

MEDLEY.
A very pretty piece of gallantry, by an eminent author, called *The Diversions of Brussels* – very necessary to be read by all old ladies who are desirous to improve themselves at questions and commands, blindman's buff, and the like fashionable recreations.

EMILIA.
Oh, ridiculous!

MEDLEY.
Then there is *The Art of Affectation*, written by a late beauty of quality, teaching you how to draw up your breasts, stretch up your neck, to thrust out your breech, to play with your head, to toss up your nose, to bite your lips, to turn up your eyes, to speak in a silly soft tone of a voice, and use all the foolish French words that will infallibly make your person and conversation charming; with a short apology at the latter end, in the behalf of young ladies who notoriously wash and paint, though they have naturally good complexions.

EMILIA.
What a deal of stuff you tell us!

MEDLEY.
Such as the town affords, madam. The Russians, hearing the great respect we have for foreign dancing, have lately sent over some of their best baladines, who are now practising a famous ballet which will be suddenly danced at the Bear Garden.

LADY TOWNLEY.
Pray forbear your idle stories, and give us an account of the state of love as it now stands.

MEDLEY.
Truly, there has been some revolutions in those affairs – great chopping and changing among the old and some new lovers, whom malice, indiscretion, and misfortune have luckily brought into play.

LADY TOWNLEY.
What think you of walking into the next room and sitting down, before you engage in this business?

MEDLEY.
I wait upon you; and I hope (though women are commonly unreasonable), by the plenty of scandal I shall discover, to give you very good content, ladies.

Exeunt

Scene Two

{*Mrs Loveit's*}

Enter Mrs Loveit and Pert. Mrs Loveit putting up a letter, then pulling out her pocket-glass and looking in it

MRS LOVEIT.
Pert.

PERT.
Madam?

MRS LOVEIT.
I hate myself, I look so ill today.

PERT.
Hate the wicked cause on't, that base man, Mr Dorimant, who makes you torment and vex yourself continually.

MRS LOVEIT.
He is to blame, indeed.

PERT.
To blame to be two days without sending, writing, or coming near you, contrary to his oath and covenant! 'Twas to much purpose to make him swear! I'll lay my life there's not an article but he has broken – talked to the vizards i' the pit, waited upon the ladies from the boxes to their coaches, gone behind the scenes and fawned upon those little insignificant creatures, the players. 'Tis impossible for a man of his inconstant temper to forbear, I'm sure.

MRS LOVEIT.
I know he is a devil, but he has something of the angel yet undefaced in him, which makes him so charming and agreeable that I must love him, be he never so wicked.

PERT.
I little thought, madam, to see your spirit tamed to this degree, who banished poor Mr Lackwit but for taking up another lady's fan in your presence.

MRS LOVEIT.
My knowing of such odious fools contributes to the making of me love Dorimant the better.

PERT.
Your knowing of Mr Dorimant, in my mind, should rather make you hate all mankind.

MRS LOVEIT.
So it does, besides himself.

PERT.
Pray, what excuse does he make in his letter?

MRS LOVEIT.
He has had business.

PERT.

Business in general terms would not have been a current excuse for another. A modish man is always very busy when he is in pursuit of a new mistress.

MRS LOVEIT.

Some fop has bribed you to rail at him. He had business; I will believe it, and will forgive him.

PERT.

You may forgive him anything, but I shall never forgive him his turning me into ridicule, as I hear he does.

MRS LOVEIT.

I perceive you are of the number of those fools his wit has made his enemies.

PERT.

I am of the number of those he's pleased to rally, madam; and if we may believe Mr Wagfan and Mr Caperwell, he sometimes makes merry with yourself, too, among his laughing companions.

MRS LOVEIT.

Blockheads are as malicious to witty men as ugly women are to the handsome; 'tis their interest, and they make it their business to defame 'em.

PERT.

I wish Mr Dorimant would not make it his business to defame you.

MRS LOVEIT.

Should he, I had rather be made infamous by him than owe my reputation to the dull discretion of those fops you talk of.

Enter Bellinda

(*Running to her*) Bellinda!

BELLINDA.

My dear!

MRS LOVEIT.

You have been unkind of late.

BELLINDA.

Do not say unkind, say unhappy.

MRS LOVEIT.

I could chide you. Where have you been these two days?

BELLINDA.

Pity me rather, my dear, where I have been so tired with two or three country gentlewomen, whose conversation has been more insufferable than a country fiddle.

MRS LOVEIT.

Are they relations?

BELLINDA.

No, Welsh acquaintance I made when I was last year at St Winifred's. They have asked me a thousand questions of the modes and intrigues of the town, and I have told 'em almost as many things for news that hardly were so when their gowns were in fashion.

MRS LOVEIT.

Provoking creatures, how could you endure 'em?

BELLINDA (*aside*)

Now to carry on my plot; nothing but love could make me capable of so much falsehood. 'Tis time to begin, lest Dorimant should come before her jealousy has stung her. (*Laughs, and then speaks on*) I was yesterday at a play with 'em, where I was fain to show 'em the living, as the man at Westminster does the dead. That is Mrs Such-a-one, admired for her beauty; this is Mr Such-a-one, cried up for a wit; that is sparkish Mr Such-a-one, who keeps reverend Mrs Such-a-one; and there sits fine Mrs Such-a-one, who was lately cast off by my Lord Such-a-one.

MRS LOVEIT.

Did you see Dorimant there?

BELLINDA.

I did, and imagine you were there with him and have no mind to own it.

MRS LOVEIT.

What should make you think so?

BELLINDA.

A lady masked, in a pretty dishabille, whom Dorimant entertained with more respect than the gallants do a common vizard.

MRS LOVEIT (*aside*)

Dorimant at the play entertaining a mask! Oh, heavens!

BELLINDA (*aside*)

Good!

MRS LOVEIT.

Did he stay all the while?

BELLINDA.

Till the play was done, and then led her out, which confirms me it was you.

MRS LOVEIT.
Traitor!

PERT.
Now you may believe he had business, and you may forgive him too.

MRS LOVEIT.
Ungrateful, perjured man!

BELLINDA.
You seem so much concerned, my dear, I fear I have told you unawares what I had better have concealed for your quiet.

MRS LOVEIT.
What manner of shape had she?

BELLINDA.
Tall and slender. Her motions were very genteel. Certainly she must be some person of condition.

MRS LOVEIT.
Shame and confusion be ever in her face when she shows it!

BELLINDA.
I should blame your discretion for loving that wild man, my dear – but they say he has a way so bewitching that few can defend their hearts who know him.

MRS LOVEIT.
I will tear him from mine, or die i' the attempt!

BELLINDA.
Be more moderate.

MRS LOVEIT.
Would I had daggers, darts, or poisoned arrows in my breast, so I could but remove the thoughts of him from thence!

BELLINDA.
Fie, fie, your transports are too violent, my dear. This may be but an accidental gallantry, and 'tis likely ended at her coach.

PERT.
Should it proceed farther, let your comfort be, the conduct Mr Dorimant affects will quickly make you know your rival – ten to one let you see her ruined, her reputation exposed to the town – a happiness none will envy her but yourself, madam.

MRS LOVEIT.
Whoe'er she be, all the harm I wish her is, may she love him as well as I do, and may he give her as much cause to hate him!

PERT.
Never doubt the latter end of your curse, madam!

MRS LOVEIT.
May all the passions that are raised by neglected love – jealousy, indignation, spite, and thirst of revenge – eternally rage in her soul, as they do now in mine!

Walks up and down with a distracted air.
Enter a Page

PAGE.
Madam, Mr Dorimant –

MRS LOVEIT.
I will not see him.

PAGE.
I told him you were within, madam.

MRS LOVEIT.
Say you lied, say I'm busy, shut the door – say anything!

PAGE.
He's here, madam.

{*Exit Page*}

Enter Dorimant.

DORIMANT.
'They taste of death who do at heaven arrive,
But we this paradise approach alive'.
(*To Mrs Loveit*) What, dancing the galloping nag without a fiddle? (*Offers to catch her by the hand; she flings away and walks on*) I fear this restlessness of the body, madam, (*pursuing her*) proceeds from an unquietness of the mind. What unlucky accident puts you out of humour – a point ill-washed, knots spoiled i' the making up, hair shaded awry, or some other little mistake in setting you in order?

PERT.
A trifle, in my opinion, sir, more inconsiderable than any you mention.

DORIMANT.
Oh, Mrs Pert! I never knew you sullen enough to be silent. Come, let me know the business.

PERT.
The business, sir, is the business that has taken you up these two days. How have I seen you laugh at men of business, and now to become a man of business yourself!

DORIMANT.

We are not masters of our own affections; our inclinations daily alter. Now we love pleasure, and anon we shall dote on business. Human frailty will have it so, and who can help it?

MRS LOVEIT.

Faithless, inhuman, barbarous man –

DORIMANT {*aside*}

Good. Now the alarm strikes –

MRS LOVEIT.

– Without sense of love, of honour, or of gratitude! Tell me, for I will know, what devil masked she was, you were with at the play yesterday.

DORIMANT.

Faith, I resolved as much as you, but the devil was obstinate and would not tell me.

MRS LOVEIT.

False in this as in your vows to me! You do know!

DORIMANT.

The truth is, I did all I could to know.

MRS LOVEIT.

And dare you own it to my face? Hell and furies!

Tears her fan in pieces

DORIMANT.

Spare your fan, madam. You are growing hot and will want it to cool you.

MRS LOVEIT.

Horror and distraction seize you, sorrow and remorse gnaw your soul, and punish all your perjuries to me!

Weeps

DORIMANT (*turning to Bellinda*)

'So thunder breaks the cloud in twain,
And makes a passage for the rain'.
(*To Bellinda*) Bellinda, you are the devil that have raised this storm. You were at the play yesterday and have been making discoveries to your dear.

BELLINDA.

You're the most mistaken man i' the world.

DORIMANT.

It must be so, and here I vow revenge – resolve to pursue and persecute you more impertinently than ever any loving fop did his mistress, hunt you i' the Park, trace you i' the Mall, dog you in every visit you make, haunt you at the plays and i' the drawing room, hang my nose in your neck and talk to you whether you will or no, and ever look upon you with such dying eyes till your friends grow jealous of me, send you out of town, and the world suspect your reputation. (*In a lower voice*) – At my Lady Townley's when we go from hence –

He looks kindly on Bellinda

BELLINDA.

– I'll meet you there.

DORIMANT.

Enough.

MRS LOVEIT (*pushing Dorimant away*)

Stand off! You shan't stare upon her so!

DORIMANT {*aside*}

Good! There's one made jealous already.

MRS LOVEIT.

Is this the constancy you vowed?

DORIMANT.

Constancy at my years? 'Tis not a virtue in season; you might as well expect the fruit the autumn ripens i' the spring.

MRS LOVEIT.

Monstrous principle!

DORIMANT.

Youth has a long journey to go, madam. Should I have set up my rest at the first inn I lodged at, I should never have arrived at the happiness I now enjoy.

MRS LOVEIT.

Dissembler, damned dissembler!

DORIMANT.

I am so, I confess. Good nature and good manners corrupt me. I am honest in my inclinations and would not, wer't not to avoid offence, make a lady a little in years believe I think her young, wilfully mistake art for nature, and seem as fond of a thing I am weary of as when I doted on't in earnest.

MRS LOVEIT.

False man!

DORIMANT.

True woman.

MRS LOVEIT.

Now you begin to show yourself!

DORIMANT.

Love gilds us over and makes us show fine things to one another for a time, but soon the gold wears off, and then again the native brass appears.

MRS LOVEIT.

Think on your oaths, your vows, and protestations, perjured man!

DORIMANT.

I made 'em when I was in love.

MRS LOVEIT.

And therefore ought they not to bind? Oh, impious!

DORIMANT.

What we swear at such a time may be a certain proof of a present passion; but to say truth, in love there is no security to be given for the future.

MRS LOVEIT.

Horrid and ungrateful, begone! And never see me more!

DORIMANT.

I am not one of those troublesome coxcombs who, because they were once well-received, take the privilege to plague a woman with their love ever after. I shall obey you, madam, though I do myself some violence.

He offers to go, and Mrs Loveit pulls him back

MRS LOVEIT.

Come back, you shan't go! Could you have the ill nature to offer it?

DORIMANT.

When love grows diseased, the best thing we can do is to put it to a violent death. I cannot endure the torture of a lingering and consumptive passion.

MRS LOVEIT.

Can you think mine sickly?

DORIMANT.

Oh, 'tis desperately ill! What worse symptoms are there than your being always uneasy when I visit you, your picking quarrels with me on slight occasions, and in my absence kindly listening to the impertinences of every fashionable fool that talks to you?

MRS LOVEIT.

What fashionable fool can you lay to my charge?

DORIMANT.

Why, the very cock-fool of all those fools, Sir Fopling Flutter.

MRS LOVEIT.

I never saw him in my life but once.

DORIMANT.

The worse woman you, at first sight to put on all your charms, to entertain him with that softness in your voice and all that wanton kindness in your eyes you so notoriously affect when you design a conquest.

MRS LOVEIT.

So damned a lie did never malice yet invent. Who told you this?

DORIMANT.

No matter. That ever I should love a woman that can dote on a senseless caper, a tawdry French ribbon, and a formal cravat.

MRS LOVEIT.

You make me mad!

DORIMANT.

A guilty conscience may do much! Go on, be the game-mistress of the town and enter all our young fops, as fast as they come from travel.

MRS LOVEIT.

Base and scurrilous!

DORIMANT.

A fine mortifying reputation 'twill be for a woman of your pride, wit, and quality!

MRS LOVEIT.

This jealousy's a mere pretence, a cursed trick of your own devising. I know you.

DORIMANT.

Believe it and all the ill of me you can. I would not have a woman have the least good thought of me that can think well of Fopling. Farewell. Fall to, and much good may do you with your coxcomb.

MRS LOVEIT.

Stay! Oh stay, and I will tell you all.

DORIMANT.

I have been told too much already.

Exit Dorimant

MRS LOVEIT.

Call him again!

PERT.

E'en let him go. A fair riddance!

MRS LOVEIT.

Run, I say! Call him again, I will have him called!

PERT.

The devil should carry him away first, were it my concern.

Exit Pert

BELLINDA.

He's frighted me from the very thoughts of loving men. For heaven's sake, my dear, do not discover what I told you. I dread his tongue as much as you ought to have done his friendship.

Enter Pert

PERT.

He's gone, madam.

MRS LOVEIT.

Lightning blast him!

PERT.

When I told him you desired him to come back, he smiled, made a mouth at me, flung into his coach, and said –

MRS LOVEIT.

What did he say?

PERT.

'Drive away' – and then repeated verses.

MRS LOVEIT.

Would I had made a contract to be a witch when first I entertained this greater devil. Monster, barbarian! I could tear myself in pieces. Revenge, nothing but revenge can ease me. Plague, war, famine, fire – all that can bring universal ruin and misery on mankind – with joy I'd perish to have you in my power but this moment!

Exit Mrs Loveit

PERT.

Follow, madam. Leave her not in this outrageous passion.

Pert gathers up the things

BELLINDA.

He's given me the proof which I desired of his love, but 'tis a proof of his ill nature too. I wish I had not seen him use her so:

I sigh to think that Dorimant may be
One day as faithless and unkind to me.

Exeunt

ACT THREE

Scene One

Lady Woodvill's lodgings

Enter Harriet and Busy, her woman

BUSY.
Dear madam! Let me set that curl in order.

HARRIET.
Let me alone. I will shake 'em all out of order!

BUSY.
Will you never leave this wildness?

HARRIET.
Torment me not.

BUSY.
Look! There's a knot falling off.

HARRIET.
Let it drop.

BUSY.
But one pin, dear madam.

HARRIET.
How do I daily suffer under thy officious fingers!

BUSY.
Ah, the difference that is between you and my Lady Dapper!
How uneasy she is if the least thing be amiss about her!

HARRIET.
She is indeed most exact. Nothing is ever wanting to make her
ugliness remarkable.

BUSY.
Jeering people say so.

HARRIET.
Her powdering, painting, and her patching never fail in
public to draw the tongues and eyes of all the men upon
her.

BUSY.
She is indeed a little too pretending.

HARRIET.
That women should set up for beauty as much in spite of
nature as some men have done for wit!

BUSY.
I hope without offence one may endeavour to make one's self
agreeable.

HARRIET.
Not when 'tis impossible. Women then ought to be no more
fond of dressing than fools should be of talking. Hoods and
modesty, masks and silence, things that shadow and conceal –
they should think of nothing else.

BUSY.
Jesu! Madam, what will your mother think is become of you?
For heaven's sake, go in again.

HARRIET.
I won't.

BUSY.
This is the extravagant'st thing that ever you did in your life,
to leave her and a gentleman who is to be your husband.

HARRIET.
My husband! Hast thou so little wit to think I spoke what I
meant when I overjoyed her in the country with a low curtsy
and 'What you please, madam; I shall ever be obedient'?

BUSY.
Nay, I know not, you have so many fetches.

HARRIET.
And this was one, to get her up to London. Nothing else, I
assure thee.

BUSY.
Well, the man, in my mind, is a fine man!

HARRIET.
The man indeed wears his clothes fashionably and has a
pretty, negligent way with him, very courtly and much
affected. He bows, and talks, and smiles so agreeably, as he
thinks.

BUSY.
I never saw anything so genteel.

HARRIET.
Varnished over with good breeding many a blockhead makes
a tolerable show.

BUSY.
I wonder you do not like him.

HARRIET.
I think I might be brought to endure him, and that is all a

reasonable woman should expect in a husband; but there is duty i' the case, and like the haughty Merab, I
'Find much aversion in my stubborn mind',
which
'Is bred by being promised and designed'.

BUSY.
I wish you do not design your own ruin! I partly guess your inclinations, madam. That Mr Dorimant –

HARRIET.
Leave your prating and sing some foolish song or other.

BUSY.
I will – the song you love so well ever since you saw Mr Dorimant.

SONG
When first Amintas charmed my heart,
My heedless sheep began to stray;
The wolves soon stole the greatest part,
And all will now be made a prey.

Ah, let not love your thoughts possess,
'Tis fatal to a shepherdess;
The dang'rous passion you must shun,
Or else like me be quite undone.

HARRIET.
Shall I be paid down by a covetous parent for a purchase? I need no land. No, I'll lay myself out all in love. It is decreed –

Enter Young Bellair

YOUNG BELLAIR.
What generous resolution are you making, madam?

HARRIET.
Only to be disobedient, sir.

YOUNG BELLAIR.
Let me join hands with you in that.

HARRIET.
With all my heart. I never thought I should have given you mine so willingly. Here, {*they join hands*} – I, Harriet –

YOUNG BELLAIR.
And I, Harry –

HARRIET.
Do solemnly protest –

YOUNG BELLAIR.
And vow –

HARRIET.
That I with you –

YOUNG BELLAIR.
And I with you –

HARRIET, YOUNG BELLAIR.
Will never marry.

HARRIET.
A match!

YOUNG BELLAIR.
And no match! How do you like this indifference now?

HARRIET.
You expect I should take it ill, I see.

YOUNG BELLAIR.
'Tis not unnatural for you women to be a little angry you miss a conquest – though you would slight the poor man were he in your power.

HARRIET.
There are some, it may be, have an eye like Bart'lomew, big enough for the whole fair, but I am not of the number, and you may keep your gingerbread. 'Twill be more acceptable to the lady whose dear image it wears, sir.

YOUNG BELLAIR.
I must confess, madam, you came a day after the fair.

HARRIET.
You own then you are in love?

YOUNG BELLAIR.
I do.

HARRIET.
The confidence is generous, and in return I could almost find in my heart to let you know my inclinations.

YOUNG BELLAIR.
Are you in love?

HARRIET.
Yes – with this dear town, to that degree I can scarce endure the country in landscapes and in hangings.

YOUNG BELLAIR.
What a dreadful thing 'twould be to be hurried back to Hampshire!

HARRIET.
Ah! Name it not!

YOUNG BELLAIR.
As for us, I find we shall agree well enough. Would we could do something to deceive the grave people!

HARRIET.
Could we delay their quick proceeding, 'twere well. A reprieve is a good step towards the getting of a pardon.

YOUNG BELLAIR.
If we give over the game, we are undone. What think you of playing it on booty?

HARRIET.
What do you mean?

YOUNG BELLAIR.
Pretend to be in love with one another. 'Twill make some dilatory excuses we may feign pass the better.

HARRIET.
Let us do't, if it be but for the dear pleasure of dissembling.

YOUNG BELLAIR.
Can you play your part?

HARRIET.
I know not what it is to love, but I have made pretty remarks by being now and then where lovers meet. Where did you leave their gravities?

YOUNG BELLAIR.
I' the next room. Your mother was censuring our modern gallant.

Enter Old Bellair and Lady Woodvill

HARRIET.
Peace! Here they come. I will lean against this wall and look bashfully down upon my fan, while you, like an amorous spark, modishly entertain me.

LADY WOODVILL {*to Old Bellair*}
Never go about to excuse 'em. Come, come, it was not so when I was a young woman.

OLD BELLAIR.
Adod, they're something disrespectful –

LADY WOODVILL.
Quality was then considered, and not rallied by every fleering fellow.

OLD BELLAIR.
Youth will have its jest, adod it will.

LADY WOODVILL.
'Tis good breeding now to be civil to none but players and Exchange women. They are treated by 'em as much above their condition as others are below theirs.

OLD BELLAIR.
Out a pize on 'em! Talk no more: the rogues ha' got an ill habit of preferring beauty, no matter where they find it.

LADY WOODVILL.
See, your son and my daughter. They have improved their acquaintance since they were within!

OLD BELLAIR.
Adod, methinks they have! Let's keep back and observe.

YOUNG BELLAIR {*to Harriet*}.
Now for a look and gestures that may persuade 'em I am saying all the passionate things imaginable.

HARRIET.
Your head a little more on one side. Ease yourself on your left leg and play with your right hand.

YOUNG BELLAIR.
Thus, is it not?

HARRIET.
Now set your right leg firm on the ground, adjust your belt, then look about you.

YOUNG BELLAIR.
A little exercising will make me perfect.

HARRIET.
Smile, and turn to me again very sparkish.

YOUNG BELLAIR.
Will you take your turn and be instructed?

HARRIET.
With all my heart.

YOUNG BELLAIR.
At one motion play your fan, roll your eyes, and then settle a kind look upon me.

HARRIET.
So.

YOUNG BELLAIR.
Now spread your fan, look down upon it, and tell the sticks with a finger.

HARRIET.
Very modish.

YOUNG BELLAIR.
Clap your hand up to your bosom, hold down your gown. Shrug a little, draw up your breasts and let 'em fall again, gently, with a sigh or two, etc.

HARRIET.
By the good instructions you give, I suspect you for one of those malicious observers who watch people's eyes and from innocent looks make scandalous conclusions.

YOUNG BELLAIR.
I know some, indeed, who out of mere love to mischief are as vigilant as jealousy itself, and will give you an account of every glance that passes at a play and i' the Circle.

HARRIET.
'Twill not be amiss now to seem a little pleasant.

YOUNG BELLAIR.
Clap your fan then in both your hands, snatch it to your mouth, smile, and with a lively motion fling your body a little forwards. So, – now spread it, fall back on the sudden, cover your face with it, and break out into a loud laughter. – Take up! Look grave, and fall a-fanning of yourself. Admirably well acted!

HARRIET.
I think I am pretty apt at these matters.

OLD BELLAIR {to Lady Woodvill}
Adod, I like this well.

LADY WOODVILL.
This promises something.

OLD BELLAIR {coming forward}
Come, there is love i' the case, adod there is, or will be. – What say you, young lady?

HARRIET.
All in good time, sir. You expect we should fall to and love as gamecocks fight, as soon as we are set together. Adod, you're unreasonable!

OLD BELLAIR.
Adod, sirrah, I like thy wit well.

Enter a Servant

SERVANT.
The coach is at the door, madam.

OLD BELLAIR.
Go, get you and take the air together.

LADY WOODVILL.
Will not you go with us?

OLD BELLAIR.
Out a pize! Adod, I ha' business and cannot. We shall meet at night at my sister Townley's.

YOUNG BELLAIR (aside).
He's going to Emilia. I overheard him talk of a collation.

Exeunt

Scene Two

{Lady Townley's house}

Enter Lady Townley, Emilia, and Medley

LADY TOWNLEY.
I pity the young lovers we last talked of, though to say truth, their conduct has been so indiscreet they deserve to be unfortunate.

MEDLEY.
You have an exact account, from the great lady i' the box down to the little orange-wench.

EMILIA.
You're a living libel, a breathing lampoon. I wonder you are not torn in pieces.

MEDLEY.
What think you of setting up an office of intelligence for these matters? The project may get money.

LADY TOWNLEY.
You would have great dealings with country ladies.

MEDLEY.
More than Muddiman has with their husbands.

Enter Bellinda

LADY TOWNLEY.
Bellinda, what has been become of you? We have not seen you here of late with your friend Mrs Loveit.

BELLINDA.
Dear creature, I left her but now so sadly afflicted.

LADY TOWNLEY.
With her old distemper, jealousy?

MEDLEY.
Dorimant has played her some new prank.

BELLINDA.
Well, that Dorimant is certainly the worst man breathing.

EMILIA.
I once thought so.

BELLINDA.
And do you not think so still?

EMILIA.
No, indeed.

BELLINDA.
Oh, Jesu!

EMILIA.
The town does him a great deal of injury, and I will never believe what it says of a man I do not know again, for his sake.

BELLINDA.
You make me wonder.

LADY TOWNLEY.
He's a very well-bred man.

BELLINDA.
But strangely ill-natured.

EMILIA.
Then he's a very witty man.

BELLINDA.
But a man of no principles.

MEDLEY.
Your man of principles is a very fine thing, indeed!

BELLINDA.
To be preferred to men of parts by women who have regard to their reputation and quiet. Well, were I minded to play the fool, he should be the last man I'd think of.

MEDLEY.
He has been the first in many ladies' favours, though you are so severe, madam.

LADY TOWNLEY.
What he may be for a lover, I know not, but he's a very pleasant acquaintance, I am sure.

BELLINDA.
Had you seen him use Mrs Loveit as I have done, you would never endure him more.

EMILIA.
What, he has quarrelled with her again?

BELLINDA.
Upon the slightest occasion. He's jealous of Sir Fopling.

LADY TOWNLEY.
She never saw him in her life but yesterday, and that was here.

EMILIA.
On my conscience, he's the only man in town that's her aversion. How horribly out of humour she was all the while he talked to her!

BELLINDA.
And somebody has wickedly told him –

EMILIA.
Here he comes.

Enter Dorimant

MEDLEY.
Dorimant, you are luckily come to justify yourself. Here's a lady –

BELLINDA.
– Has a word or two to say to you from a disconsolate person.

DORIMANT.
You tender your reputation too much, I know, madam, to whisper with me before this good company.

BELLINDA.
To serve Mrs Loveit, I'll make a bold venture.

DORIMANT.
Here's Medley, the very spirit of scandal.

BELLINDA.
No matter!

EMILIA.
'Tis something you are unwilling to hear, Mr Dorimant.

LADY TOWNLEY.
Tell him, Bellinda, whether he will or no.

BELLINDA (*aloud*)
Mrs Loveit –

DORIMANT.
Softly, these are laughers. You do not know 'em.

BELLINDA (*to Dorimant, apart*)
In a word, you've made me hate you, which I thought you never could have done.

DORIMANT.
In obeying your commands.

BELLINDA.
'Twas a cruel part you played. How could you act it?

DORIMANT.
Nothing is cruel to a man who could kill himself to please you. Remember, five o'clock tomorrow morning.

BELLINDA.
I tremble when you name it.

DORIMANT.
Be sure you come.

BELLINDA.
I shan't.

DORIMANT.
Swear you will.

BELLINDA.
I dare not.

DORIMANT.
Swear, I say!

BELLINDA.
By my life, by all the happiness I hope for –

DORIMANT.
You will.

BELLINDA.
I will.

DORIMANT.
Kind.

BELLINDA.
I am glad I've sworn. I vow I think I should ha' failed you else.

DORIMANT.
Surprisingly kind! In what temper did you leave Loveit?

BELLINDA.
Her raving was prettily over, and she began to be in a brave

way of defying you and all your works. Where have you been since you went from thence?

DORIMANT.
I looked in at the play.

BELLINDA.
I have promised and must return to her again.

DORIMANT.
Persuade her to walk in the Mall this evening.

BELLINDA.
She hates the place and will not come.

DORIMANT.
Do all you can to prevail with her.

BELLINDA.
For what purpose?

DORIMANT.
Sir Fopling will be here anon. I'll prepare him to set upon her there before me.

BELLINDA.
You persecute her too much. But I'll do all you'll ha' me.

DORIMANT (*aloud*)
Tell her plainly, 'tis grown so dull a business I can drudge on no longer.

EMILIA.
There are afflictions in love, Mr Dorimant.

DORIMANT.
You women make 'em, who are commonly as unreasonable in that as you are at play: without the advantage be on your side, a man can never quietly give over when he's weary.

MEDLEY.
If you would play without being obliged to complaisance, Dorimant, you should play in public places.

DORIMANT.
Ordinaries were a very good thing for that, but gentlemen do not of late frequent 'em. The deep play is now in private houses.

Bellinda offering to steal away

LADY TOWNLEY.
Bellinda, are you leaving us so soon?

BELLINDA.
I am to go to the Park with Mrs Loveit, madam.

{*Exit Bellinda*}

LADY TOWNLEY.
This confidence will go nigh to spoil this young creature.

MEDLEY.
'Twill do her good, madam. Young men who are brought up under practising lawyers prove the abler counsel when they come to be called to the bar themselves.

DORIMANT.
The town has been very favourable to you this afternoon, my Lady Townley. You used to have an *embarras* of chairs and coaches at your door, an uproar of footmen in your hall, and a noise of fools above here.

LADY TOWNLEY.
Indeed, my house is the general rendezvous and, next to the playhouse, is the common refuge of all the young idle people.

EMILIA.
Company is a very good thing, madam, but I wonder you do not love it a little more chosen.

LADY TOWNLEY.
'Tis good to have an universal taste. We should love wit, but for variety be able to divert ourselves with the extravagancies of those who want it.

MEDLEY.
Fools will make you laugh.

EMILIA.
For once or twice – but the repetition of their folly after a visit or two grows tedious and insufferable.

LADY TOWNLEY.
You are a little too delicate, Emilia.

Enter a Page

PAGE.
Sir Fopling Flutter, madam, desires to know if you are to be seen.

LADY TOWNLEY.
Here's the freshest fool in town, and one who has not cloyed you yet. – Page!

PAGE.
Madam?

LADY TOWNLEY.
Desire him to walk up.

{*Exit Page*}

DORIMANT.
Do not you fall on him, Medley, and snub him. Soothe him up in his extravagance. He will show the better.

MEDLEY.
You know I have a natural indulgence for fools and need not this caution, sir.

Enter Sir Fopling, with his Page after him

SIR FOPLING.
Page, wait without.

{*Exit Page*}

{*to Lady Townley*} Madam, I kiss your hands. I see yesterday was nothing of chance; the *belles assemblées* form themselves here every day. (*To Emilia*) Lady, your servant. – Dorimant, let me embrace thee. Without lying, I have not met with any of my acquaintance who retain so much of Paris as thou dost – the very air thou hadst when the marquise mistook thee i' the Tuileries and cried, '*Hé chevalier!*' and then begged thy pardon.

DORIMANT.
I would fain wear in fashion as long as I can, sir. 'Tis a thing to be valued in men as well as baubles.

SIR FOPLING.
Thou art a man of wit and understands the town. Prithee, let thee and I be intimate. There is no living without making some good man the *confident* of our pleasures.

DORIMANT.
'Tis true – but there is no man so improper for such a business as I am.

SIR FOPLING.
Prithee, why hast thou so modest an opinion of thyself?

DORIMANT.
Why, first, I could never keep a secret in my life; and then, there is no charm so infallibly makes me fall in love with a woman as my knowing a friend loves her. I deal honestly with you.

SIR FOPLING.
Thy humour's very gallant, or let me perish. I knew a French count so like thee.

LADY TOWNLEY.

Wit, I perceive, has more power over you than beauty, Sir Fopling, else you would not have let this lady stand so long neglected.

SIR FOPLING (*to Emilia*)

A thousand pardons, madam, – some civilities due of course upon the meeting a long absent friend. The *éclat* of so much beauty, I confess, ought to have charmed me sooner.

EMILIA.

The *brillant* of so much good language, sir, has much more power than the little beauty I can boast.

SIR FOPLING.

I never saw anything prettier than this high work on your *point d'Espagne*.

EMILIA.

'Tis not so rich as *point de Venise*.

SIR FOPLING.

Not altogether, but looks cooler, and is more proper for the season. – Dorimant, is not that Medley?

DORIMANT.

The same, sir.

SIR FOPLING {*to Medley*}

Forgive me, sir; in this *embarras* of civilities I could not come to have you in my arms sooner. You understand an equipage the best of any man in town, I hear.

MEDLEY.

By my own you would not guess it.

SIR FOPLING.

There are critics who do not write, sir.

MEDLEY.

Our peevish poets will scarce allow it.

SIR FOPLING.

Damn 'em, they'll allow no man wit who does not play the fool like themselves and show it! Have you taken notice of the gallesh I brought over?

MEDLEY.

Oh, yes! 'T has quite another air than the English makes.

SIR FOPLING.

'Tis as easily known from an English tumbril as an Inns of Court man is from one of us.

DORIMANT.

Truly there is a *bel air* in galleshes as well as men.

MEDLEY.

But there are few so delicate to observe it.

SIR FOPLING.

The world is generally very *grossier* here, indeed.

LADY TOWNLEY {(*to Emilia*}

He's very fine.

EMILIA.

Extreme proper!

SIR FOPLING.

A slight suit I made to appear in at my first arrival – not worthy your consideration, ladies.

DORIMANT.

The pantaloon is very well mounted.

SIR FOPLING.

The tassels are new and pretty.

MEDLEY.

I never saw a coat better cut.

SIR FOPLING.

It makes me show long-waisted, and, I think, slender.

DORIMANT.

That's the shape our ladies dote on.

MEDLEY.

Your breech, though, is a handful too high, in my eye, Sir Fopling.

SIR FOPLING.

Peace, Medley, I have wished it lower a thousand times, but a pox on 't, 'twill not be!

LADY TOWNLEY.

His gloves are well fringed, large, and graceful.

SIR FOPLING.

I was always eminent for being *bien ganté*.

EMILIA.

He wears nothing but what are originals of the most famous hands in Paris.

SIR FOPLING.

You are in the right, madam.

LADY TOWNLEY.

The suit?

SIR FOPLING.
Barroy.

EMILIA.
The garniture?

SIR FOPLING.
Le Gras.

MEDLEY.
The shoes?

SIR FOPLING.
Piccar.

DORIMANT.
The periwig?

SIR FOPLING.
Chedreux.

LADY TOWNLEY, EMILIA.
The gloves?

SIR FOPLING.
Orangerie – you know the smell, ladies. – Dorimant, I could find in my heart for an amusement to have a gallantry with some of our English ladies.

DORIMANT.
'Tis a thing no less necessary to confirm the reputation of your wit than a duel will be to satisfy the town of your courage.

SIR FOPLING.
Here was a woman yesterday –

DORIMANT.
Mrs Loveit.

SIR FOPLING.
You have named her!

DORIMANT.
You cannot pitch on a better for your purpose.

SIR FOPLING.
Prithee, what is she?

DORIMANT.
A person of quality, and one who has a rest of reputation enough to make the conquest considerable. Besides I hear she likes you too.

SIR FOPLING.
Methoughts she seemed, though, very reserved and uneasy all the time I entertained her.

DORIMANT.
Grimace and affectation! You will see her i' the Mall tonight.

SIR FOPLING.
Prithee, let thee and I take the air together.

DORIMANT.
I am engaged to Medley, but I'll meet you at St James's and give you some information upon the which you may regulate your proceedings.

SIR FOPLING.
All the world will be in the Park tonight. – Ladies, 'twere pity to keep so much beauty longer within doors and rob the Ring of all those charms that should adorn it. – Hey, page!

Enter Page

See that all my people be ready.

{Page} goes out again

Dorimant, *à revoir.*

Exit Sir Fopling

MEDLEY.
A fine-mettled coxcomb.

DORIMANT.
Brisk and insipid –

MEDLEY.
Pert and dull.

EMILIA.
However you despise him, gentlemen, I'll lay my life he passes for a wit with many.

DORIMANT.
That may very well be. Nature has her cheats, stums a brain, and puts sophisticate dullness often on the tasteless multitude for true wit and good humour. – Medley, come.

MEDLEY.
I must go a little way. I will meet you i' the Mall.

DORIMANT.
I'll walk through the garden thither. (*To the women*) We shall meet anon and bow.

LADY TOWNLEY.
Not tonight. We are engaged about a business, the knowledge of which may make you laugh hereafter.

MEDLEY.

Your servant, ladies.

DORIMANT.

À revoir, as Sir Fopling says.

{*Exeunt Medley and Dorimant*}

LADY TOWNLEY.

The old man will be here immediately.

EMILIA.

Let's expect him i' the garden.

LADY TOWNLEY.

Go, you are a rogue!

EMILIA.

I can't abide you!

Exeunt

Scene Three

The Mall

Enter Harriet and Young Bellair, she pulling him

HARRIET.

Come along!

YOUNG BELLAIR.

And leave your mother?

HARRIET.

Busy will be sent with a hue and cry after us; but that's no matter.

YOUNG BELLAIR.

'Twill look strangely in me.

HARRIET.

She'll believe it a freak of mine and never blame your manners.

YOUNG BELLAIR {*pointing*}

What reverend acquaintance is that she has met?

HARRIET.

A fellow beauty of the last king's time, though by the ruins you would hardly guess it.

Exeunt

Enter Dorimant and crosses the stage
Enter Young Bellair and Harriet

YOUNG BELLAIR.

By this time your mother is in a fine taking.

HARRIET.

If your friend Mr Dorimant were but here now, that she might find me talking with him!

YOUNG BELLAIR.

She does not know him but dreads him, I hear, of all mankind.

HARRIET.

She concludes if he does but speak to a woman, she's undone – is on her knees every day to pray heaven defend me from him.

YOUNG BELLAIR.

You do not apprehend him so much as she does?

HARRIET.

I never saw anything in him that was frightful.

YOUNG BELLAIR.

On the contrary, have you not observed something extreme delightful in his wit and person?

HARRIET.

He's agreeable and pleasant, I must own, but he does so much affect being so, he displeases me.

YOUNG BELLAIR.

Lord, madam, all he does and says is so easy and so natural.

HARRIET.

Some men's verses seem so to the unskilful; but labour i' the one and affectation in the other to the judicious plainly appear.

YOUNG BELLAIR.

I never heard him accused of affectation before.

Enter Dorimant and stares upon her

HARRIET.

It passes on the easy town, who are favourably pleased in him to call it humour.

{*Exeunt Young Bellair and Harriet*}

DORIMANT.

'Tis she! It must be she – that lovely hair, that easy shape, those wanton eyes, and all those melting charms about her mouth which Medley spoke of. I'll follow the lottery and put in for a prize with my friend Bellair.

{Exit Dorimant, repeating} –

'In love the victors from the vanquished fly;
They fly that wound, and they pursue that die'.

Enter Young Bellair and Harriet, and after them Dorimant, standing at a distance

YOUNG BELLAIR.
Most people prefer Hyde Park to this place.

HARRIET.
It has the better reputation, I confess; but I abominate the dull diversions there – the formal bows, the affected smiles, the silly by-words and amorous tweers in passing. Here one meets with a little conversation now and then.

YOUNG BELLAIR.
These conversations have been fatal to some of your sex, madam.

HARRIET.
It may be so. Because some who want temper have been undone by gaming, must others who have it wholly deny themselves the pleasure of play?

DORIMANT (*coming up gently and bowing to her*)
Trust me, it were unreasonable, madam.

HARRIET.
Lord! Who's this?

She starts and looks grave

YOUNG BELLAIR.
Dorimant.

DORIMANT.
Is this the woman your father would have you marry?

YOUNG BELLAIR.
It is.

DORIMANT.
Her name?

YOUNG BELLAIR.
Harriet.

DORIMANT *{aside}*
I am not mistaken. – She's handsome.

YOUNG BELLAIR.
Talk to her; her wit is better than her face. We were wishing for you but now.

DORIMANT (*to Harriet*)
Overcast with seriousness o' the sudden! A thousand smiles were shining in that face but now – I never saw so quick a change of weather.

HARRIET (*aside*)
I feel as great a change within, but he shall never know it.

DORIMANT.
You were talking of play, madam. Pray, what may be your stint?

HARRIET.
A little harmless discourse in public walks, or at most an appointment in a box, barefaced, at the playhouse. You are for masks and private meetings, where women engage for all they are worth, I hear.

DORIMANT.
I have been used to deep play, but I can make one at small game when I like my gamester well.

HARRIET.
And be so unconcerned you'll ha' no pleasure in 't.

DORIMANT.
Where there is a considerable sum to be won, the hope of drawing people in makes every trifle considerable.

HARRIET.
The sordidness of men's natures, I know, makes 'em willing to flatter and comply with the rich, though they are sure never to be the better for 'em.

DORIMANT.
'Tis in their power to do us good, and we despair not but at some time or other they may be willing.

HARRIET.
To men who have fared in this town like you, 'twould be a great mortification to live on hope. Could you keep a Lent for a mistress?

DORIMANT.
In expectation of a happy Easter, and though time be very precious, think forty days well lost to gain your favour.

HARRIET.
Mr Bellair! Let us walk. 'Tis time to leave him. Men grow dull when they begin to be particular.

DORIMANT.

You're mistaken. Flattery will not ensue, though I know you're greedy of the praises of the whole Mall.

HARRIET.

You do me wrong.

DORIMANT.

I do not. As I followed you, I observed how you were pleased when the fops cried 'She's handsome, very handsome, by God she is!' and whispered aloud your name – the thousand several forms you put your face into; then, to make yourself more agreeable, how wantonly you played with your head, flung back your locks, and looked smilingly over your shoulder at 'em.

HARRIET.

I do not go begging the men's, as you do the ladies' good liking, with a sly softness in your looks and a gentle slowness in your bows as you pass by 'em. As thus, sir – (*Acts him*) Is not this like you?

Enter Lady Woodvill and Busy

YOUNG BELLAIR.

Your mother, madam!

Pulls Harriet. She composes herself

LADY WOODVILL.

Ah, my dear child Harriet!

BUSY {*aside*}

Now is she so pleased with finding her again, she cannot chide her.

LADY WOODVILL.

Come away!

DORIMANT.

'Tis now but high Mall, madam – the most entertaining time of all the evening.

HARRIET.

I would fain see that Dorimant, mother, you so cry out of for a monster. He's in the Mall, I hear.

LADY WOODVILL.

Come away, then! The plague is here, and you should dread the infection.

YOUNG BELLAIR.

You may be misinformed of the gentleman.

LADY WOODVILL.

Oh no! I hope you do not know him. He is the prince of all the devils in the town – delights in nothing but in rapes and riots.

DORIMANT.

If you did but hear him speak, madam –

LADY WOODVILL.

Oh, he has a tongue, they say, would tempt the angels to a second fall.

Enter Sir Fopling with his equipage, six footmen and a page

SIR FOPLING.

Hey, Champagne, Norman, La Rose, La Fleur, La Tour, La Verdure! – Dorimant! –

LADY WOODVILL.

Here, here he is among this rout! He names him! – Come away, Harriet, come away!

Exeunt Lady Woodvill, Harriet, Busy, and Young Bellair

DORIMANT {*aside*}

This fool's coming has spoiled all. She's gone, but she has left a pleasing image of herself behind that wanders in my soul. – It must not settle there.

SIR FOPLING.

What reverie is this? Speak, man.

DORIMANT.

'Snatched from myself, how far behind
Already I behold the shore!'

Enter Medley

MEDLEY.

Dorimant, a discovery! I met with Bellair –

DORIMANT.

You can tell me no news, sir. I know all.

MEDLEY.

How do you like the daughter?

DORIMANT.

You never came so near truth in your life as you did in her description.

MEDLEY.

What think you of the mother?

DORIMANT.

Whatever I think of her, she thinks very well of me, I find.

MEDLEY.
Did she know you?

DORIMANT.
She did not. Whether she does now or no, I know not. Here was a pleasant scene towards, when in came Sir Fopling, mustering up his equipage, and at the latter end named me and frighted her away.

MEDLEY.
Loveit and Bellinda are not far off. I saw 'em alight at St James's.

DORIMANT
Sir Fopling, hark you, a word of two. (*Whispers*) – Look you do not want assurance.

SIR FOPLING.
I never do on these occasions.

DORIMANT.
Walk on, we must not be seen together. Make your advantage of what I have told you. The next turn you will meet the lady.

SIR FOPLING.
Hey! Follow me all.

Exeunt Sir Fopling and his equipage

DORIMANT.
Medley, you shall see good sport anon between Loveit and this Fopling.

MEDLEY.
I thought there was something toward, by that whisper.

DORIMANT.
You know a worthy principle of hers?

MEDLEY.
Not to be so much as civil to a man who speaks to her in the presence of him she professes to love.

DORIMANT.
I have encouraged Fopling to talk to her tonight.

MEDLEY.
Now you are here, she will go nigh to beat him.

DORIMANT.
In the humour she's in, her love will make her do some very extravagant thing, doubtless.

MEDLEY.
What was Bellinda's business with you at my Lady Townley's?

DORIMANT.
To get me to meet Loveit here in order to an *éclaircissement*. I made some difficulty of it and have prepared this rencounter to made good my jealousy.

MEDLEY.
Here they come.

Enter Mrs Loveit, Bellinda, and Pert

DORIMANT.
I'll meet her and provoke her with a deal of dumb civility in passing by, then turn short and be behind her when Sir Fopling sets upon her – {*Bows to Mrs Loveit*}
  'See how unregarded now
  That piece of beauty passes'.

Exeunt Dorimant and Medley

BELLINDA.
How wonderful respectfully he bowed!

PERT.
He's always over-mannerly when he has done a mischief.

BELLINDA.
Methoughts, indeed, at the same time he had a strange, despising countenance.

PERT.
The unlucky look he thinks becomes him.

BELLINDA.
I was afraid you would have spoke to him, my dear.

MRS LOVEIT.
I would have died first. He shall no more find me the loving fool he has done.

BELLINDA.
You love him still!

MRS LOVEIT.
No.

PERT.
I wish you did not.

MRS LOVEIT.
I do not, and I will have you think so! – What made you hale me to this odious place, Bellinda?

BELLINDA.
I hate to be hulched up in a coach. Walking is much better.

MRS LOVEIT.
Would we could meet Sir Fopling now!

BELLINDA.
Lord, would you not avoid him?

MRS LOVEIT.
I would make him all the advances that may be.

BELLINDA.
That would confirm Dorimant's suspicion, my dear.

MRS LOVEIT.
He is not jealous, but I will make him so, and be revenged a way he little thinks on.

BELLINDA (*aside*)
If she should make him jealous, that may make him fond of her again. I must dissuade her from it. – Lord, my dear, this will certainly make him hate you.

MRS LOVEIT.
'Twill make him uneasy, though he does not care for me. I know the effects of jealousy on men of his proud temper.

BELLINDA.
'Tis a fantastic remedy: its operations are dangerous and uncertain.

MRS LOVEIT.
'Tis the strongest cordial we can give to dying love. It often brings it back when there's no sign of life remaining. But I design not so much the reviving his, as my revenge.

Enter Sir Fopling and his equipage

SIR FOPLING.
Hey! Bid the coachman send home four of his horses and bring the coach to Whitehall. I'll walk over the Park. {*To Mrs Loveit*} Madam, the honour of kissing your fair hands is a happiness I missed this afternoon at my Lady Townley's.

MRS LOVEIT.
You were very obliging, Sir Fopling, the last time I saw you there.

SIR FOPLING.
The preference was due to your wit and beauty. {*To Bellinda*} Madam, your servant. There never was so sweet an evening.

BELLINDA.
'T has drawn all the rabble of the town hither.

SIR FOPLING.
'Tis pity there's not an order made that none but the *beau monde* should walk here.

MRS LOVEIT.
'Twould add much to the beauty of the place. See what a sort of nasty fellows are coming!

Enter four ill-fashioned fellows singing:
    "Tis not for kisses alone, etc.'

MRS LOVEIT.
Foh! Their periwigs are scented with tobacco so strong –

SIR FOPLING.
– It overcomes our pulvilio. Methinks I smell the coffee-house they come from.

FIRST MAN.
Dorimant's convenient, Madame Loveit.

SECOND MAN.
I like the oily buttock with her.

THIRD MAN {*pointing to Sir Fopling*}
What spruce prig is that?

FIRST MAN.
A caravan, lately come from Paris.

SECOND MAN.
Peace, they smoke!

All of them coughing
    'There's something else to be done, etc.'

                                            Exeunt singing

Enter Dorimant and Medley

DORIMANT.
They're engaged –

MEDLEY.
She entertains him as if she liked him.

DORIMANT.
Let us go forward, seem earnest in discourse, and show ourselves. Then you shall see how she'll use him.

BELLINDA.
Yonder's Dorimant, my dear.

MRS LOVEIT.
I see him. (*Aside*) He comes insulting, but I will disappoint him in his expectation. (*To Sir Fopling*) – I like this pretty, nice humour of yours, Sir Fopling. {*To Bellinda*} With what a loathing eye he looked upon those fellows!

SIR FOPLING.
I sat near one of 'em at a play today and was almost poisoned with a pair of cordovan gloves he wears.

MRS LOVEIT.
Oh, filthy cordovan! How I hate the smell!

Laughs in a loud, affected way

SIR FOPLING.
Did you observe, madam, how their cravats hung loose an inch from their neck, and what a frightful air it gave 'em?

MRS LOVEIT.
Oh! I took particular notice of one that is always spruced up with a deal of dirty, sky-coloured ribbon.

BELLINDA.
That's one of the walking flageolets who haunt the Mall o' nights.

MRS LOVEIT.
Oh, I remember him! He has a hollow tooth, enough to spoil the sweetness of an evening.

SIR FOPLING.
I have seen the tallest walk the streets with a dainty pair of boxes, neatly buckled on.

MRS LOVEIT.
And a little footboy at his heels, pocket-high, with a flat cap, a dirty face –

SIR FOPLING.
– And a snotty nose.

MRS LOVEIT.
Oh, odious! There's many of my own sex, with that Holborn equipage, trig to Gray's Inn Walks, and now and then travel hither on a Sunday.

MEDLEY {*to Dorimant*}.
She takes no notice of you.

DORIMANT.
Damn her! I am jealous of a counterplot.

MRS LOVEIT.
Your liveries are the finest, Sir Fopling. Oh, that page! that page is the prettily'st dressed. They are all Frenchmen?

SIR FOPLING.
There's one damned English blockhead among 'em. You may know him by his mien.

MRS LOVEIT.
Oh, that's he, that's he! What do you call him?

SIR FOPLING {*calling Footman*}
Hey! – I know not what to call him.

MRS LOVEIT.
What's your name?

FOOTMAN.
John Trott, madam.

SIR FOPLING.
Oh, insufferable! Trott, Trott, Trott! There's nothing so barbarous as the names of our English servants. What countryman are you, sirrah?

FOOTMAN.
Hampshire, sir.

SIR FOPLING.
Then Hampshire be your name. Hey, Hampshire!

MRS LOVEIT.
Oh, that sound! That sound becomes the mouth of a man of quality.

MEDLEY.
Dorimant, you look a little bashful on the matter.

DORIMANT.
She dissembles better than I thought she could have done.

MEDLEY.
You have tempted her with too luscious a bait. She bites at the coxcomb.

DORIMANT.
She cannot fall from loving me to that?

MEDLEY.
You begin to be jealous in earnest.

DORIMANT.
Of one I do not love?

MEDLEY.
You did love her.

DORIMANT.
The fit has long been over.

MEDLEY.
But I have known men fall into dangerous relapses when they have found a woman inclining to another.

DORIMANT (*to himself*)
He guesses the secret of my heart. I am concerned but dare not show it, lest Bellinda should mistrust all I have done to gain her.

BELLINDA (*aside*)
I have watched his look and find no alteration there. Did he love her, some signs of jealousy would have appeared.

DORIMANT {*to Mrs Loveit*}
I hope this happy evening, madam, has reconciled you to the scandalous Mall. We shall have you now hankering here again.

MRS LOVEIT.
Sir Fopling, will you walk?

SIR FOPLING.
I am all obedience, madam.

MRS LOVEIT.
Come along then, and let's agree to be malicious on all the ill-fashioned things we meet.

SIR FOPLING.
We'll make a critique on the whole Mall, madam.

MRS LOVEIT.
Bellinda, you shall engage –

BELLINDA.
To the reserve of our friends, my dear.

MRS LOVEIT.
No! No exceptions.

SIR FOPLING.
We'll sacrifice all to our diversion.

MRS LOVEIT.
All – all –

SIR FOPLING.
All!

BELLINDA.
All? Then let it be.

Exeunt Sir Fopling, Mrs Loveit, Bellinda, and Pert, laughing

MEDLEY.
Would you had brought some more of your friends, Dorimant, to have been witnesses of Sir Fopling's disgrace and your triumph!

DORIMANT.
'Twere unreasonable to desire you not to laugh at me, but pray do not expose me to the town this day or two.

MEDLEY.
By that time you hope to have regained your credit?

DORIMANT.
I know she hates Fopling and only makes use of him in hope to work me on again. Had it not been for some powerful considerations which will be removed tomorrow morning, I had made her pluck off this mask and show the passion that lies panting under.

Enter a Footman

MEDLEY.
Here comes a man from Bellair, with news of your last adventure.

DORIMANT.
I am glad he sent him. I long to know the consequence of our parting.

FOOTMAN.
Sir, my master desires you to come to my Lady Townley's presently and bring Mr Medley with you. My Lady Woodvill and her daughter are there.

MEDLEY.
Then all's well, Dorimant.

FOOTMAN.
They have sent for the fiddles and mean to dance. He bid me tell you, sir, the old lady does not know you, and would have you own yourself to be Mr Courtage. They are all prepared to receive you by that name.

DORIMANT.
That foppish admirer of quality, who flatters the very meat at honourable tables and never offers love to a woman below a lady-grandmother!

MEDLEY.
You know the character you are to act, I see.

DORIMANT.
This is Harriet's contrivance – wild, witty, lovesome, beautiful, and young. – Come along, Medley.

MEDLEY.

This new woman would well supply the loss of Loveit.

DORIMANT.

That business must not end so. Before tomorrow sun is set, I will revenge and clear it.

And you and Loveit, to her cost, shall find
I fathom all the depths of womankind.

Exeunt

ACT FOUR

Scene One

{*Lady Townley's house*}

The scene opens with the fiddles playing a country dance

Enter Dorimant {and} Lady Woodvill, Young Bellair and Mrs Harriet, Old Bellair and Emilia, Mr Medley and Lady Townley, as having just ended the dance

OLD BELLAIR.

So, so, so! A smart bout, a very smart bout, adod!

LADY TOWNLEY.

How do you like Emilia's dancing, brother?

OLD BELLAIR.

Not at all, not at all!

LADY TOWNLEY.

You speak not what you think, I am sure.

OLD BELLAIR.

No matter for that – go, bid her dance no more. It don't become her, it don't become her. Tell her I say so. (*Aside*) Adod, I love her.

DORIMANT (*to Lady Woodvill*)

All people mingle nowadays, madam. And in public places women of quality have the least respect showed 'em.

LADY WOODVILL.

I protest you say the truth, Mr Courtage.

DORIMANT.

Forms and ceremonies, the only things that uphold quality and greatness, are now shamefully laid aside and neglected.

LADY WOODVILL.

Well, this is not the women's age, let 'em think what they will. Lewdness is the business now; love was the business in my time.

DORIMANT.

The women, indeed, are little beholding to the young men of this age. They're generally only dull admirers of themselves and make their court to nothing but their periwigs and their cravats – and would be more concerned for the disordering of 'em, though on a good occasion, than a young maid would be for the tumbling of her head or handkercher.

LADY WOODVILL.
I protest you hit 'em.

DORIMANT.
They are very assiduous to show themselves at court, well-dressed, to the women of quality; but their business is with the stale mistresses of the town, who are prepared to receive their lazy addresses by industrious old lovers who have cast 'em off and made 'em easy.

HARRIET {to Medley}
He fits my mother's humour so well, a little more and she'll dance a kissing dance with him anon.

MEDLEY.
Dutifully observed, madam.

DORIMANT.
They pretend to be great critics in beauty – by their talk you would think they liked no face – and yet can dote on an ill one if it belong to a laundress or a tailor's daughter. They cry a woman's past her prime at twenty, decayed at four-and-twenty, old and insufferable at thirty.

LADY WOODVILL.
Insufferable at thirty! That they are in the wrong, Mr Courtage, at five-and-thirty there are living proofs enough to convince 'em.

DORIMANT.
Ay, madam! There's Mrs Setlooks, Mrs Droplip, and my Lady Loud. Show me among all our opening buds a face that promises so much beauty as the remains of theirs.

LADY WOODVILL.
The depraved appetite of this vicious age tastes nothing but green fruit and loathes it when 'tis kindly ripened.

DORIMANT.
Else so many deserving women, madam, would not be so untimely neglected.

LADY WOODVILL.
I protest, Mr Courtage, a dozen such good men as you would be enough to atone for that wicked Dorimant and all the under-debauchees of the town. (Mrs Harriet, Emilia, Young Bellair, Medley {and} Lady Townley break out into a laughter) – What's the matter there?

MEDLEY.
A pleasant mistake, madam, that a lady has made, occasions a little laughter.

OLD BELLAIR {to Dorimant and Lady Woodvill}
Come, come, you keep 'em idle! They are impatient till the fiddles play again.

DORIMANT.
You are not weary, madam?

LADY WOODVILL.
One dance more. I cannot refuse you, Mr Courtage.

They dance. After the dance, Old Bellair singing and dancing up to Emilia

EMILIA.
You are very active, sir.

OLD BELLAIR.
Adod, sirrah, when I was a young fellow, I could ha' capered up to my woman's gorget.

DORIMANT (to Lady Woodvill}
You are willing to rest yourself, madam?

LADY TOWNLEY {to Dorimant and Lady Woodvill}
We'll walk into my chamber and sit down.

MEDLEY.
Leave us Mr Courtage; he's a dancer, and the young ladies are not weary yet.

LADY WOODVILL.
We'll send him out again.

HARRIET.
If you do not quickly, I know where to send for Mr Dorimant.

LADY WOODVILL.
This girl's head, Mr Courtage, is ever running on that wild fellow.

DORIMANT.
'Tis well you have got her a good husband, madam. That will settle it.

Exeunt Lady Townley, Lady Woodvill, and Dorimant

OLD BELLAIR (to Emilia)
Adod, sweetheart, be advised and do not throw thyself away on a young idle fellow.

EMILIA.
I have no such intention, sir.

OLD BELLAIR.
Have a little patience! Thou shalt have the man I spake of.

Adod, he loves thee and will make a good husband. But no words –

EMILIA.
But, sir –

OLD BELLAIR.
No answer – out a pize! Peace, and think on 't.

Enter Dorimant

DORIMANT.
Your company is desired within, sir.

OLD BELLAIR.
I go, I go! Good Mr Courtage, fare you well. (*To Emilia*) Go, I'll see you no more!

EMILIA.
What have I done, sir?

OLD BELLAIR.
You are ugly, you are ugly! – Is she not, Mr Courtage?

EMILIA.
Better words, or I shan't abide you!

OLD BELLAIR.
Out a pize! Adod, what does she say – Hit her a pat for me there.

Exit Old Bellair

MEDLEY {*to Dorimant*}
You have charms for the whole family.

DORIMANT.
You'll spoil all with some unseasonable jest, Medley.

MEDLEY.
You see I confine my tongue and am content to be a bare spectator, much contrary to my nature.

EMILIA.
Methinks, Mr Dorimant, my Lady Woodvill is a little fond of you.

DORIMANT.
Would her daughter were.

MEDLEY.
It may be you may find her so. Try her. You have an opportunity.

DORIMANT.
And I will not lose it. – Bellair, here's a lady has something to say to you.

YOUNG BELLAIR.
I wait upon her. – Mr Medley, we have both business with you.

DORIMANT.
Get you all together, then. {*He bows to Harriet; she curtsies*} (*To Harriet*) That demure curtsy is not amiss in jest, but do not think in earnest it becomes you.

HARRIET.
Affectation is catching, I find. From your grave bow I got it.

DORIMANT.
Where had you all that scorn and coldness in your look?

HARRIET.
From nature, sir – pardon my want of art. I have not learnt those softnesses and languishings which now in faces are so much in fashion.

DORIMANT.
You need 'em not. You have a sweetness of your own, if you would but calm your frowns and let it settle.

HARRIET.
My eyes are wild and wandering like my passions, and cannot yet be tied to rules of charming.

DORIMANT.
Women, indeed, have commonly a method of managing those messengers of love. Now they will look as if they would kill, and anon they will look as if they were dying. They point and rebate their glances, the better to invite us.

HARRIET.
I like this variety well enough, but hate the set face that always looks as it would say, 'Come love me' – a woman who at plays makes the *doux yeux* to a whole audience and at home cannot forbear 'em to her monkey.

DORIMANT.
Put on a gentle smile and let me see how well it will become you.

HARRIET.
I am sorry my face does not please you as it is, but I shall not be complaisant and change it.

DORIMANT.

Though you are obstinate, I know 'tis capable of improvement, and shall do you justice, madam, if I chance to be at court when the critics of the circle pass their judgment – for thither you must come.

HARRIET.

And expect to be taken in pieces, have all my features examined, every motion censured, and on the whole be condemned to be but pretty – or a beauty of the lowest rate. What think you?

DORIMANT.

The women – nay, the very lovers who belong to the drawing room – will maliciously allow you more than that. They always grant what is apparent, that they may the better be believed when they name concealed faults they cannot easily be disproved in.

HARRIET.

Beauty runs as great a risk exposed at court as wit does on the stage, where the ugly and the foolish all are free to censure.

DORIMANT (*aside*)

I love her and dare not let her know it. I fear she has an ascendant o'er me and may revenge the wrongs I have done her sex. (*To her*:) Think of making a party, madam; love will engage.

HARRIET.

You make me start! I did not think to have heard of love from you.

DORIMANT.

I never knew what 'twas to have a settled ague yet, but now and then have had irregular fits.

HARRIET.

Take heed, sickness after long health is commonly more violent and dangerous.

DORIMANT (*aside*)

I have took the infection from her and feel the disease now spreading in me. (*To her*) Is the name of love so frightful that you dare not stand it?

HARRIET.

'Twill do little execution out of your mouth on me, I am sure.

DORIMANT.

It has been fatal –

HARRIET.

To some easy women, but we are not all born to one destiny. I was informed you use to laugh at love, and not make it.

DORIMANT.

The time has been, but now I must speak –

HARRIET.

If it be on that idle subject, I will put on my serious look, turn my head carelessly from you, drop my lip, let my eyelids fall and hang half o'er my eyes – thus, while you buzz a speech of an hour long in my ear and I answer never a word. Why do you not begin?

DORIMANT.

That the company may take notice how passionately I make advances of love and how disdainfully you receive 'em.

HARRIET.

When your love's grown strong enough to make you bear being laughed at, I'll give you leave to trouble me with it. Till when, pray forbear, sir.

Enter Sir Fopling and others in masks

DORIMANT.

What's here – masquerades?

HARRIET.

I thought that foppery had been left off, and people might have been in private with a fiddle.

DORIMANT.

'Tis endeavoured to be kept on foot still by some who find themselves the more acceptable the less they are known.

YOUNG BELLAIR.

This must be Sir Fopling.

MEDLEY.

That extraordinary habit shows it.

YOUNG BELLAIR.

What are the rest?

MEDLEY.

A company of French rascals whom he picked up in Paris and has brought over to be his dancing equipage on these occasions. Make him own himself; a fool is very troublesome when he presumes he is incognito.

SIR FOPLING (*to Harriet*)

Do you know me?

HARRIET.
Ten to one but I guess at you.

SIR FOPLING.
Are you women as fond of a vizard as we men are?

HARRIET.
I am very fond of a vizard that covers a face I do not like, sir.

YOUNG BELLAIR.
Here are no masks, you see, sir, but those which came with you. This was intended a private meeting, but because you look like a gentleman, if you will discover yourself and we know you to be such, you shall be welcome.

SIR FOPLING (*pulling off his mask*)
Dear Bellair!

MEDLEY.
Sir Fopling! How come you hither?

SIR FOPLING.
Faith, as I was coming late from Whitehall, after the King's couchée, one of my people told me he had heard fiddles at my Lady Townley's, and –

DORIMANT.
You need not say any more, sir.

SIR FOPLING.
Dorimant, let me kiss thee.

DORIMANT.
Hark you, Sir Fopling –

Whispers

SIR FOPLING.
Enough, enough, Courtage. – {*Looking at Harriet*} A pretty kind of young woman that, Medley. I observed her in the Mall, more *éveillée* than our English women commonly are. Prithee, what is she?

MEDLEY.
The most noted coquette in town. Beware of her.

SIR FOPLING.
Let her be what she will, I know how to take my measures. In Paris the mode is to flatter the *prude*, laugh at the *faux-prude*, make serious love to the *demi-prude*, and only rally with the *coquette*. Medley, what think you?

DORIMANT.
That for all this smattering of the mathematics, you may be

out in your judgment at tennis

SIR FOPLING.
What a *coq-à-l'âne* is this? I talk of women, and thou answerest tennis.

MEDLEY.
Mistakes will be, for want of apprehension.

SIR FOPLING.
I am very glad of the acquaintance I have with this family.

MEDLEY.
My lady truly is a good woman.

SIR FOPLING.
Ah, Dorimant – Courtage, I would say – would thou hadst spent the last winter in Paris with me. When thou wert there, La Corneus and Sallyes were the only *habitudes* we had; a comedian would have been a *bonne fortune*. No stranger ever passed his time so well as I did some moths before I came over. I was well received in a dozen families, where all the women of quality used to visit. I have intrigues to tell thee more pleasant than ever thou read'st in a novel.

HARRIET.
Write 'em, sir, and oblige us women. Our language wants such little stories.

SIR FOPLING.
Writing, madam, 's a mechanic part of wit. A gentleman should never go beyond a song or a *billet*.

HARRIET.
Bussy was a gentleman.

SIR FOPLING.
Who, d'Ambois?

MEDLEY {*aside*}
Was there ever such a brisk blockhead?

HARRIET.
Not d'Ambois, sir, but Rabutin – he who writ the *Loves of France*.

SIR FOPLING.
That may be, madam! Many gentlemen do things that are below 'em. – Damn your authors, Courtage, women are the prettiest thing we can fool away our time with.

HARRIET.
I hope ye have wearied yourself tonight at court, sir, and will not think of fooling with anybody here.

SIR FOPLING.

I cannot complain of my fortune there, madam. – Dorimant –

DORIMANT.

Again!

SIR FOPLING.

Courtage, a pox on 't! I have something to tell thee. When I had made my court within, I came out and flung myself upon the mat under the state i' the outward room, i' the midst of half a dozen beauties who were withdrawn to jeer among themselves, as they called it.

DORIMANT.

Did you know 'em?

SIR FOPLING.

Not one of 'em, by heavens, not I! But they were all your friends.

DORIMANT.

How are you sure of that?

SIR FOPLING.

Why, we laughed at all the town – spared nobody but yourself. They found me a man for their purpose.

DORIMANT.

I know you are malicious to your power.

SIR FOPLING.

And, faith, I had occasion to show it, for I never saw more gaping fools at a ball or on a Birthday.

DORIMANT.

You learned who the women were?

SIR FOPLING.

No matter ! – they frequent the drawing room.

DORIMANT.

And entertain themselves pleasantly at the expense of all the fops who come there.

SIR FOPLING.

That's their business. Faith, I sifted 'em and find they have a sort of wit among them. (*Pinches a tallow candle*) – Ah, filthy!

DORIMANT.

Look, he has been pinching the tallow candle.

SIR FOPLING.

How can you breathe in a room where there's grease frying?

Dorimant, thou art intimate with my lady – advise her, for her own sake and the good company that comes hither, to burn wax lights.

HARRIET.

What are these masquerades who stand so obsequiously at a distance?

SIR FOPLING.

A set of baladines, whom I picked out of the best in France and brought over with a flute douce or two – my servants. They shall entertain you.

HARRIET.

I had rather see you dance yourself, Sir Fopling.

SIR FOPLING.

And I had rather do it – all the company knows it. But, madam –

MEDLEY.

Come, come! No excuses, Sir Fopling!

SIR FOPLING.

By heavens, Medley –

MEDLEY.

Like a woman I find you must be struggled with before one brings you to what you desire.

HARRIET (*aside*)

Can de dance?

EMILIA.

And fence and sing too, if you'll believe him.

DORIMANT.

He has no more excellence in his heels than in his head. He went to Paris a plain, bashful English blockhead, and is returned a fine, undertaking French fop.

MEDLEY {*to Harriet*}

I cannot prevail.

SIR FOPLING.

Do not think it want of complaisance, madam.

HARRIET.

You are too well-bred to want that, Sir Fopling. I believe it want of power.

SIR FOPLING.

By heavens, and so it is! I have sat up so damned late and drunk so cursed hard since I came to this lewd town that I am fit for nothing but low dancing now – a *courante*, a *bourrée*, or a *menuet*. But St André tells me, if I will but be regular, in one month I shall rise again. (*Endeavours at a caper*) – Pox on this debauchery!

EMILIA.
I have heard your dancing much commended.

SIR FOPLING.
It had the good fortune to please in Paris. I was judged to rise within an inch as high as the Basque in an entry I danced there.

HARRIET {*to Emilia*}.
I am mightily taken with this fool. Let us sit. – Here's a seat, Sir Fopling.

SIR FOPLING.
At your feet madam. I can be nowhere so much at ease. – By your leave, gown. {*Sits*}

HARRIET, EMILIA.
Ah, you'll spoil it!

SIR FOPLING.
No matter, my clothes are my creatures. I make 'em to make my court to you ladies. – Hey! *qu'on commence!*

Dance

(*To {John Trott, one of the dancers}*) – English motions! I was forced to entertain this fellow, one of my set miscarrying. – Oh, horrid! Leave your damned manner of dancing and put on the French air. Have you not a pattern before you? {*Dances*} – Pretty well! Imitation in time may bring him to something.

After the dance, enter Old Bellair, Lady Woodvill, and Lady Townley

OLD BELLAIR.
Hey, adod, what have we here? A mumming?

LADY WOODVILL.
Where's my daughter? – Harriet!

DORIMANT.
Here, here, madam. I know not but under these disguises there may be dangerous sparks. I gave the young lady warning.

LADY WOODVILL.
Lord! I am so obliged to you Mr Courtage.

HARRIET.
Lord! How you admire this man!

LADY WOODVILL.
What have you to except against him?

HARRIET.
He's a fop.

LADY WOODVILL.
He's not a Dorimant, a wild, extravagant fellow of the times.

HARRIET.
He's a man made up of forms and commonplaces, sucked out of the remaining lees of the last age.

LADY WOODVILL.
He's so good a man that were you not engaged –

LADY TOWNLEY.
You'll have but little night to sleep in.

LADY WOODVILL.
Lord! 'tis perfect day –

DORIMANT (*aside*)
The hour is almost come I appointed Bellinda, and I am not so foppishly in love here to forget. I am flesh and blood yet.

LADY TOWNLEY.
I am very sensible, madam.

LADY WOODVILL.
Lord, madam –

HARRIET.
Look in what a struggle is my poor mother yonder!

YOUNG BELLAIR.
She has much ado to bring out the compliment.

DORIMANT.
She strains hard for it.

HARRIET.
See, see – her head tottering, her eyes staring, and her underlip trembling.

DORIMANT.
Now, now she's in the very convulsions of her civility. (*Aside*) – 'Sdeath, I shall lose Bellinda! I must fright her hence. She'll be an hour in this fit of good manners else. (*To Lady Woodvill*) Do you not know Sir Fopling, madam?

LADY WOODVILL.
I have seen that face. Oh heaven! – 'tis the same we met in the Mall! How came he here?

DORIMANT.

A fiddle in this town is a kind of fop-call. No sooner it strikes up, but the house is besieged with an army of masquerades straight.

LADY WOODVILL.

Lord, I tremble, Mr Courtage! For certain Dorimant is in the company.

DORIMANT.

I cannot confidently say he is not. You had best begone; I will wait upon you. Your daughter is in the hands of Mr Bellair.

LADY WOODVILL.

I'll see her before me. – Harriet, come away!

{*Exeunt Lady Woodvill and Harriet*}

YOUNG BELLAIR.

Lights, lights!

LADY TOWNLEY.

Light, down there!

OLD BELLAIR.

Adod, it needs not –

{*Exeunt Lady Townley, Emilia and Young Bellair*}

DORIMANT {*calling to servants outside*}

Call my Lady Woodvill's coach to the door, quickly.

{*Exit Dorimant*}

OLD BELLAIR.

Stay, Mr Medley, let the young fellows do that duty. We will drink a glass of wine together. 'Tis good after dancing. {*Looks at Sir Fopling*} – What mumming spark is that?

MEDLEY.

He is not to be comprehended in few words.

SIR FOPLING.

Hey, La Tour!

MEDLEY.

Whither away, Sir Fopling?

SIR FOPLING.

I have business with Courtage.

MEDLEY.

He'll but put the ladies into their coach and come up again.

OLD BELLAIR.

In the meantime I'll call for a bottle.

{*Exit Old Bellair*}

Enter Young Bellair

MEDLEY.

Where's Dorimant?

YOUNG BELLAIR.

Stolen home. He has had business waiting for him there all this night, I believe, by an impatience I observed in him.

MEDLEY.

Very likely. 'Tis but dissembling drunkenness, railing at his friends, and the kind soul will embrace the blessing and forget the tedious expectation.

SIR FOPLING.

I must speak with him before I sleep.

YOUNG BELLAIR {*to Medley*}

Emilia and I are resolved on that business.

MEDLEY.

Peace, here's your father.

Enter Old Bellair and butler with a bottle of wine.

OLD BELLAIR.

The women are all gone to bed. – Fill, boy! – Mr Medley, begin a health.

MEDLEY (*whispers*)

To Emilia.

OLD BELLAIR.

Out a pize! She's a rogue, and I'll not pledge you.

MEDLEY.

I know you will.

OLD BELLAIR.

Adod, drink it, then!

SIR FOPLING.

Let us have the new *bachique*.

OLD BELLAIR.

Adod, that is a hard word! What does it mean, sir?

MEDLEY.

A catch or drinking song.

OLD BELLAIR.

Let us have it, then!

SIR FOPLING.
Fill the glasses round, and draw up in a body. – Hey, music!

They sing

The pleasures of love and and the joys of good wine,
To perfect our happiness wisely we join.
    We to beauty all day
    Give the sovereign sway
And her favourite nymphs devoutly obey.
At the plays we are constantly making our court,
And when they are ended, we follow the sport
    To the Mall and the Park
    Where we love till 'tis dark.
    Then sparkling champagne
    Puts an end to their reign:
    It quickly recovers
    Poor languishing lovers,
Makes us frolic and gay, and drowns all our sorrow;
But alas, we relapse again on the morrow.
    Let every man stand
    With his glass in his hand,
And briskly discharge at the word of command.
    Here's a health to all those
    Whom tonight we depose.
Wine and beauty by turns great souls should inspire;
Present all together – and now, boys, give fire!

{*They drink*}

OLD BELLAIR.
Adod, a pretty business and very merry!

SIR FOPLING.
Hark you, Medley, let you and I take the fiddles and go waken Dorimant.

MEDLEY.
We shall do him a courtesy, if it be as I guess. For after the fatigue of this night, he'll quickly have his belly full and be glad of an occasion to cry, 'Take away, Handy!'

YOUNG BELLAIR.
I'll go with you; and there we'll consult about affairs, Medley.

OLD BELLAIR.
Adod, 'tis six o'clock!

SIR FOPLING.
Let's away, then.

OLD BELLAIR.
Mr Medley, my sister tell me you are an honest man. And, adod, I love you. – Few words and hearty, that's the way with old Harry, old Harry.

SIR FOPLING {*to his servants*}
Light your flambeaux! Hey!

OLD BELLAIR.
What does the man mean?

MEDLEY.
'Tis day, Sir Fopling.

SIR FOPLING.
No matter; our serenade will look the greater.

Exeunt Omnes

Scene Two

Dorimant's lodging; a table, a candle, a toilet, etc. Handy tying up linen

Enter Dorimant in his gown, and Bellinda

DORIMANT.
Why will you be gone so soon?

BELLINDA.
Why did you stay out so late?

DORIMANT.
Call a chair, Handy.

{*Exit Handy*}

– What makes you tremble so?

BELLINDA.
I have a thousand fears about me. Have I not been seen, think you?

DORIMANT.
By nobody but myself and trusty Handy.

BELLINDA.
Where are all your people?

DORIMANT.
I have dispersed 'em on sleeveless errands. What does that sigh mean?

BELLINDA.
Can you be so unkind to ask me? Well – (*sighs*) – were it to do again –

DORIMANT.
We should do it, should we not?

BELLINDA.
I think we should: the wickeder man you, to make me love so well. Will you be discreet now?

DORIMANT.
I will.

BELLINDA.
You cannot.

DORIMANT.
Never doubt it.

BELLINDA.
I will not expect it.

DORIMANT.
You do me wrong.

BELLINDA.
You have no more power to keep the secret than I had not to trust you with it.

DORIMANT.
By all the joys I have had, and those you keep in store –

BELLINDA.
– You'll do for my sake what you never did before.

DORIMANT.
By that truth thou hast spoken, a wife shall sooner betray herself to her husband.

BELLINDA.
Yet I had rather you should be false in this than in another thing you promised me.

DORIMANT.
What's that?

BELLINDA.
That you would never see Loveit more but in public places – in the Park, at court and plays.

DORIMANT.
'Tis not likely a man should be fond of seeing a damned old play when there is a new one acted.

BELLINDA.
I dare not trust your promise.

DORIMANT.
You may.

BELLINDA.
This does not satisfy me. You shall swear you never will see her more.

DORIMANT.
I will, a thousand oaths! By all –

BELLINDA.
Hold! You shall not, now I think on 't better.

DORIMANT.
I will swear!

BELLINDA.
I shall grow jealous of the oath and think I owe your truth to that, not to your love.

DORIMANT.
Then, by my love! No other oath I'll swear.

Enter Handy

HANDY.
Here's a chair.

BELLINDA.
Let me go.

DORIMANT.
I cannot.

BELLINDA.
Too willingly, I fear.

DORIMANT.
Too unkindly feared. When will you promise me again?

BELLINDA.
Not this fortnight.

DORIMANT.
You will be better than your word.

BELLINDA.
I think I shall. Will it not make you love me less?

Fiddles without

(*Starting*) Hark, what fiddles are these?

DORIMANT.
Look out, Handy.

Exit Handy and returns

HANDY.
Mr Medley, Mr Bellair, and Sir Fopling. They are coming up.

DORIMANT.
How got they in?

HANDY.
The door was open for the chair.

BELLINDA.
Lord, let me fly!

DORIMANT.
Here, here, down the back stairs. I'll see you into your chair.

BELLINDA.
No, no! Stay and receive 'em. And be sure you keep your word and never see Loveit more. Let it be a proof of your kindness.

DORIMANT.
It shall. – Handy, direct her. – (*Kissing her hand*) Everlasting love go along with thee.

Exeunt Bellinda and Handy

Enter Young Bellair, Medley, and Sir Fopling {with his page}

YOUNG BELLAIR.
Not abed yet?

MEDLEY.
You have had an irregular fit, Dorimant.

DORIMANT.
I have.

YOUNG BELLAIR.
And is it off already?

DORIMANT.
Nature has done her part, gentlemen. When she falls kindly to work, great cures are effected in little time, you know.

SIR FOPLING.
We thought there was a wench in the case, by the chair that waited. Prithee, make us a *confidence*.

DORIMANT.
Excuse me.

SIR FOPLING.
Le sage Dorimant. Was she pretty?

DORIMANT.
So pretty she may come to keep her coach and pay parish duties, if the good humour of the age continue.

MEDLEY.
And be of the number of the ladies kept by public-spirited men for the good of the whole town.

SIR FOPLING.
Well said, Medley.

Sir Fopling dancing by himself

YOUNG BELLAIR.
See Sir Fopling dancing.

DORIMANT.
You are practising and have a mind to recover, I see.

SIR FOPLING.
Prithee, Dorimant, why hast not thou a glass hung up here? A room is the dullest thing without one!

YOUNG BELLAIR.
Here is company to entertain you.

SIR FOPLING.
But I mean in case of being alone. In a glass a man may entertain himself –

DORIMANT.
The shadow of himself, indeed.

SIR FOPLING.
– Correct the errors of his motions and his dress.

MEDLEY.
I find, Sir Fopling, in your solitude you remember the saying of the wise man, and study yourself.

SIR FOPLING.
'Tis the best diversion in our retirements. Dorimant, thou art a pretty fellow and wearest thy clothes well, but I never saw thee have a handsome cravat. Were they made up like mine, they'd give another air to thy face. Prithee, let me send my man to dress thee but one day. By heavens, an Englishman cannot tie a ribbon!

DORIMANT.
They are something clumsy-fisted.

SIR FOPLING.
I have brought over the prettiest fellow that ever spread a toilet. He served some time under Mérille, the greatest *génie* in the world for a *valet de chambre*.

DORIMANT.
What, he who formerly belonged to the Duke of Candale?

SIR FOPLING.
The same, and got him his immortal reputation.

DORIMANT.
You've a very fine brandenburgh on, Sir Fopling.

SIR FOPLING.
It serves to wrap me up, after the fatigue of a ball.

MEDLEY.
I see you often in it, with your periwig tied up.

SIR FOPLING.
We should not always be in a set dress. 'Tis more *en cavalier* to appear now and then in a *déshabillé*.

MEDLEY.
Pray, how goes your business with Loveit?

SIR FOPLING.
You might have answered yourself in the Mall last night. – Dorimant, did you not see the advances she made me? I have been endeavouring at a song.

DORIMANT.
Already?

SIR FOPLING.
'Tis my *coup d'essai* in English. I would fain have thy opinion of it.

DORIMANT.
Let's see it.

SIR FOPLING.
Hey, page, give me my song. – Bellair, here. Thou hast a pretty voice, sing it.

YOUNG BELLAIR.
Sing it yourself, Sir Fopling.

SIR FOPLING.
Excuse me.

YOUNG BELLAIR.
You learnt to sing in Paris.

SIR FOPLING.
I did – of Lambert, the greatest master in the world; but I have his own fault, a weak voice, and care not to sing out of a ruelle.

DORIMANT.
A ruelle is a pretty cage for a singing fop, indeed.

Young Bellair reads the song

How charming Phillis is, how fair!
  Ah, that she were as willing
To ease my wounded heart of care,
  And make her eyes less killing.
I sigh! I sigh! I languish now,
  And love will not let me rest;
I drive about the Park and bow,
  Still as I meet my dearest.

SIR FOPLING.
Sing it, sing it, man! It goes to a pretty new tune which I am confident was made by Baptiste.

MEDLEY.
Sing it yourself, Sir Fopling. He does not know the tune.

SIR FOPLING.
I'll venture.

Sir Fopling sings

DORIMANT.
Ay, marry, now 'tis something. I shall not flatter you, Sir Fopling: there is not much though in 't, but 'tis passionate and well-turned.

MEDLEY.
After the French way.

SIR FOPLING.
That I aimed at. Does it not give you a lovely image of the thing? Slap, down goes the glass, and thus we are at it.

DORIMANT.
It does indeed. I perceive, Sir Fopling, you'll be the very head of the sparks who are lucky in compositions of this nature.

Enter Sir Fopling's Footman

SIR FOPLING.
La Tour, is the bath ready?

FOOTMAN.
Yes, sir.

SIR FOPLING.
Adieu donc, mes chers.

Exit Sir Fopling {with Footman and Page}

MEDLEY.
When have you your revenge on Loveit, Dorimant?

DORIMANT.
I will but change my linen and about it.

MEDLEY.
The powerful considerations which hindered have been removed then?

DORIMANT.
Most luckily, this morning. You must go along with me; my reputation lies at stake there.

MEDLEY.
I am engaged to Bellair.

DORIMANT.
What's your business?

MEDLEY.
Ma-tri-mony, an't like you.

DORIMANT.
It does not, sir.

YOUNG BELLAIR.
It may in time, Dorimant. What think you of Mrs Harriet?

DORIMANT.
What does she think of me?

YOUNG BELLAIR.
I am confident she loves you.

DORIMANT.
How does it appear?

YOUNG BELLAIR.
Why, she's never well but when she's talking of you, but then she finds all the faults in you she can. She laughs at all who commend you; but then she speaks ill of all who do not.

DORIMANT.
Women of her temper betray themselves by their over-cunning. I had once a growing love with a lady who would always quarrel with me when I came to see her, and yet was never quiet if I stayed a day from her.

YOUNG BELLAIR.
My father is in love with Emilia.

DORIMANT.
That is a good warrant for your proceedings. Go on and prosper – I must to Loveit. Medley, I am sorry you cannot be a witness.

MEDLEY.
Make her meet Sir Fopling again in the same place and use him ill before me.

DORIMANT.
That may be brought about, I think. – I'll be at your aunt's anon and give you joy, Mr Bellair.

YOUNG BELLAIR.
You had not best think of Mrs Harriet too much. Without church security, there's no taking up there.

DORIMANT.
I may fall into the snare, too. But,
The wise will find a difference in our fate:
You wed a woman, I a good estate.

Exeunt

Scene Three

{Outside Mrs Loveit's}

Enter the chair with Bellinda; the men set it down and open it

Bellinda starting

BELLINDA (*surprised*)
Lord, where am I? In the Mall! Whither have you brought me?

FIRST CHAIRMAN.
You gave us no directions, madam.

BELLINDA (*aside*).
The fright I was in made me forget it.

FIRST CHAIRMAN.
We use to carry a lady from the squire's hither.

BELLINDA (*aside*)
This is Loveit! I am undone if she sees me. – Quickly, carry me away!

FIRST CHAIRMAN.
Whither, an't like your honour?

BELLINDA.
Ask no questions!

Enter Mrs Loveit's Footman

FOOTMAN.
Have you seen my lady, madam?

BELLINDA.
I am just come to wait upon her.

FOOTMAN.
She will be glad to see you, madam. She sent me to you this morning to desire your company, and I was told you went out by five o'clock.

BELLINDA (*aside*)
More and more unlucky!

FOOTMAN.
Will you walk in, madam?

BELLINDA.
I'll discharge my chair and follow. Tell your mistress I am here.

{*Exit Footman*}

Take this! ({*Bellinda*} *gives the Chairmen money*) – and if ever you should be examined, be sure you say you took me up in the Strand, over against the Exchange – as you will answer it to Mr Dorimant.

CHAIRMEN.
We will, an't like your honour.

{*Exeunt Chairmen*}

BELLINDA.
Now to come off, I must on:
In confidence and lies some hopes is left;
'Twere hard to be found out in the first theft.

Exit

ACT FIVE

Scene One

{*Mrs Loveit's*}

Enter Mrs Loveit and Pert, her woman

PERT.
Well! In my eyes, Sir Fopling is no such despicable person.

MRS LOVEIT.
You are an excellent judge.

PERT.
He's as handsome a man as Mr Dorimant, and as great a gallant.

MRS LOVEIT.
Intolerable Is 't not enough I submit to his impertinences, but must I be plagued with yours too?

PERT.
Indeed, madam –

MRS LOVEIT.
'Tis false, mercenary malice –

Enter her Footman

FOOTMAN.
Mrs Bellinda, madam.

MRS LOVEIT.
What of her?

FOOTMAN.
She's below.

MRS LOVEIT.
How came she?

FOOTMAN.
In a chair – Ambling Harry brought her.

MRS LOVEIT.
He bring her! His chair stands near Dorimant's door and always brings me from thence. – Run and ask him where he took her up. Go!

{*Exit Footman*}

There is no truth in friendship neither. Women as well as men, all are false – or all are so to me at least.

PERT.
You are jealous of her too?

MRS LOVEIT.
You had best tell her I am. 'Twill become the liberty you take of late. {*Aside*} This fellow's bringing of her, her going out by five o'clock – I know not what to think.

Enter Bellinda

Bellinda, you are grown an early riser, I hear!

BELLINDA.
Do you wonder, my dear, what made me abroad so soon?

MRS LOVEIT.
You do not use to be so.

BELLINDA.
The country gentlewomen I told you of – Lord, they have the oddest diversions! – would never let me rest till I promised to go with them to the markets this morning to eat fruit and buy nosegays.

MRS LOVEIT.
Are they so fond of a filthy nosegay?

BELLINDA.
They complain of the stinks of the town and are never well but when they have their noses in one.

MRS LOVEIT.
There are essences and sweet waters.

BELLINDA.
Oh, they cry out upon perfumes, they are unwholesome. One of 'em was falling into a fit with the smell of these nerolii.

MRS LOVEIT.
Methinks, in complaisance you should have had a nosegay too.

BELLINDA.
Do you think, my dear, I could be so loathsome to trick myself up with carnations and stock-gillyflowers? I begged their pardon and told them I never wore anything but orange-flowers and tuberose. That which made me willing to go was a strange desire I had to eat some fresh nectarines.

MRS LOVEIT.
And had you any?

BELLINDA.
The best I ever tasted.

MRS LOVEIT.
Whence came you now?

BELLINDA.
From their lodgings, where I crowded out of a coach and took a chair to come and see you, my dear.

MRS LOVEIT.
Whither did you send for that chair?

BELLINDA.
'Twas going by empty.

MRS LOVEIT.
Where do these country gentlewomen lodge, I pray?

BELLINDA.
In the Strand, over against the Exchange.

PERT.
That place is never without a nest of 'em. They are always, as one goes by, fleering in balconies or staring out of windows.

Enter Footman

MRS LOVEIT (*to the Footman*)
Come hither.

Whispers

BELLINDA (*aside*).
This fellow by her order has been questioning the chairman. I threatened 'em with the name of Dorimant. If they should have told truth, I am lost forever.

MRS LOVEIT.
In the Strand, said you?

FOOTMAN.
Yes, madam, over against the Exchange.

{*Exit Footman*}

MRS LOVEIT.
She's innocent, and I am much to blame.

BELLINDA (*aside*)
I am so frightened my countenance will betray me.

MRS LOVEIT.
Bellinda, what makes you look so pale?

BELLINDA.
Want of my usual rest and jolting up and down so long in an odious hackney.

Footman returns

FOOTMAN.
Madam, Mr Dorimant.

{*Exit Footman*}

MRS LOVEIT.
What makes him here?

BELLINDA (*aside*)
Then I am betrayed indeed. He has broke his word, and I love a man that does not care for me.

MRS LOVEIT.
Lord! – you faint, Bellinda.

BELLINDA.
I think I shall – such an oppression here on the sudden.

PERT.
She has eaten too much fruit, I warrant you.

MRS LOVEIT.
Not unlikely.

PERT.
'Tis that lies heavy on her stomach.

MRS LOVEIT.
Have her into my chamber, give her some surfeit-water, and let her lie down a little.

PERT.
Come, madam. I was a strange devourer of fruit when I was young – so ravenous.

Exeunt Bellinda and Pert, leading her off

MRS LOVEIT.
Oh, that my love would be but calm awhile, that I might receive this man with all the scorn and indignation he deserves!

Enter Dorimant

DORIMANT.
Now for a touch of Sir Fopling to begin with. – Hey, page! Give positive order that none of my people stir. Let the *canaille* wait, as they should do. – Since noise and nonsense have such powerful charms,
'I, that I may successful prove,
Transform myself to what you love'.

MRS LOVEIT.
If that would do, you need not change from what you are – you can be vain and loud enough.

DORIMANT.
But not with so good a grace as Sir Fopling. – 'Hey, Hampshire!' – Oh, that sound! That sound becomes the mouth of a man of quality.

MRS LOVEIT.
Is there a thing so hateful as a senseless mimic?

DORIMANT.
He's a great grievance, indeed, to all who – like yourself, madam – love to play the fool in quiet.

MRS LOVEIT.
A ridiculous animal, who has more of the ape than the ape has of the man in him.

DORIMANT.
I have as mean an opinion of a sheer mimic as yourself; yet were he all ape, I should prefer him to the gay, the giddy, brisk, insipid, noisy fool you dote on.

MRS LOVEIT.
Those noisy fools, however you despise 'em, have good qualities which weigh more (or ought, at least) with us women than all the pernicious wit you have to boast of.

DORIMANT.
That I may hereafter have a just value for their merit, pray do me the favour to name 'em.

MRS LOVEIT.
You'll despise 'em as the dull effects of ignorance and vanity, yet I care not if I mention some. First, they really admire us, while you at best but flatter us well.

DORIMANT.
Take heed! – fools can dissemble too.

MRS LOVEIT.
They may – but not so artificially as you. There is no fear they should deceive us. Then, they are assiduous, sir. They are ever offering us their service and always waiting on our will.

DORIMANT.
You owe that to their excessive idleness. They know not how to entertain themselves at home, and find so little welcome abroad, they are fain to fly to you who countenance 'em, as a refuge against the solitude they would be otherwise condemned to.

MRS LOVEIT.
Their conversation, too, diverts us better.

DORIMANT.

Playing with your fan, smelling to your gloves, commending your hair, and taking notice how 'tis cut and shaded after the new way –

MRS LOVEIT.

Were it sillier than you can make it, you must allow 'tis pleasanter to laugh at others than to be laughed at ourselves, though never so wittily. Then, though they want skill to flatter us, they flatter themselves so well, they save us the labour. We need not take that care and pains to satisfy 'em of our love, which we so often lose on you.

DORIMANT.

They commonly, indeed, believe too well of themselves, and always better of you than you deserve.

MRS LOVEIT.

You are in the right: they have an implicit faith in us, which keeps 'em from prying narrowly into our secrets, and saves us the vexatious trouble of clearing doubts which your subtle and causeless jealousies every moment raise.

DORIMANT.

There is an inbred falsehood in women which inclines 'em still to them whom they may most easily deceive.

MRS LOVEIT.

The man who loves above his quality does not suffer more from the insolent impertinence of his mistress than the woman who loves above her understanding does from the arrogant presumptions of her friend.

DORIMANT.

You mistake the use of fools: they are designed for properties and not for friends. You have an indifferent stock of reputation left yet. Lose it all like a frank gamester on the square. 'Twill then be time enough to turn rook and cheat it up again on a good, substantial bubble.

MRS LOVEIT.

The old and the ill-favoured are only fit for properties, indeed, but young and handsome fools have met with kinder fortunes.

DORIMANT.

They have, to the shame of your sex be it spoken. 'Twas this, the thought of this, made me by a timely jealousy endeavour to prevent the good fortune you are providing for Sir Fopling. But against a woman's frailty all our care is vain.

MRS LOVEIT.

Had I not with a dear experience bought the knowledge of your falsehood, you might have fooled me yet. This is not the first jealousy you have feigned to make a quarrel with me, and get a week to throw away on some such unknown, inconsiderable slut as you have been lately lurking with at plays.

DORIMANT.

Women, when they would break off with a man, never want the address to turn the fault on him.

MRS LOVEIT.

You take a pride of late in using of me ill, that the town may know the power you have over me, which now (as unreasonably as yourself) expects that I, do me all the injuries you can, must love you still.

DORIMANT.

I am so far from expecting that you should, I begin to think you never did love me.

MRS LOVEIT.

Would the memory of it were so wholly worn out in me that I did doubt it too. What made you come to disturb my growing quiet?

DORIMANT.

To give you joy of your growing infamy.

MRS LOVEIT.

Insupportable! Insulting devil! This from you, the only author of my shame! This from another had been but justice, but from you, 'tis a hellish and inhuman outrage. What have I done?

DORIMANT.

A thing that puts you below my scorn and makes my anger as ridiculous as you have made my love.

MRS LOVEIT.

I walked last night with Sir Fopling.

DORIMANT.

You did, madam; and you talked and laughed aloud, 'Ha, ha, ha'. Oh, that laugh! That laugh becomes the confidence of a woman of quality.

MRS LOVEIT.

You, who have more pleasure in the ruin of a woman's reputation than in the endearments of her love, reproach me not with yourself – and I defy you to name the man can lay a blemish on my fame.

DORIMANT.

To be seen publicly so transported with the vain follies of that notorious fop, to me is an infamy below the sin of prostitution with another man.

MRS LOVEIT.

Rail on! I am satisfied in the justice of what I did: you had provoked me to it.

DORIMANT.

What I did was the effect of a passion whose extravagancies you have been willing to forgive.

MRS LOVEIT.

And what I did was the effect of a passion you may forgive if you think fit.

DORIMANT.

Are you so indifferent grown?

MRS LOVEIT.

I am.

DORIMANT.

Nay, then 'tis time to part. I'll send you back your letters you have so often asked for. {Looks in his pockets} I have two or three of 'em about me.

MRS LOVEIT.

Give 'em me.

DORIMANT.

You snatch as if you thought I would not. {Gives her the letters} – There. And may the perjuries in 'em be mine if e'er I see you more.

Offers to go: she catches him.

MRS LOVEIT.

Stay!

DORIMANT.

I will not.

MRS LOVEIT.

You shall!

DORIMANT.

What have you to say?

MRS LOVEIT.

I cannot speak it yet.

DORIMANT.

Something more in commendation of the fool. Death, I want patience! Let me go.

MRS LOVEIT.

I cannot. (Aside) I can sooner part with the limbs that hold him. – I hate that nauseous fool, you know I do.

DORIMANT.

Was it the scandal you were fond of, then?

MRS LOVEIT.

You had raised my anger equal to my love, a thing you ne'er could do before; and in revenge I did – I know not what I did. Would you would not think on't any more.

DORIMANT.

Should I be willing to forget it, I shall be daily minded of it. 'Twill be a commonplace for all the town to laugh at me, and Medley, when he is rhetorically drunk, will ever be declaiming on it in my ears.

MRS LOVEIT.

'Twill be believed a jealous spite! Come, forget it.

DORIMANT.

Let me consult my reputation; you are too careless of it. (Pauses) You shall meet Sir Fopling in the Mall again tonight.

MRS LOVEIT.

What mean you?

DORIMANT.

I have thought on it, and you must. 'Tis necessary to justify my love to the world. You can handle a coxcomb as he deserves when you are not out of humour, madam.

MRS LOVEIT.

Public satisfaction for the wrong I have done you! This is some new device to make me more ridiculous.

DORIMANT.

Hear me.

MRS LOVEIT.

I will not.

DORIMANT.

You will be persuaded.

MRS LOVEIT.

Never!

DORIMANT.

Are you so obstinate?

MRS LOVEIT.

Are you so base?

DORIMANT.
You will not satisfy my love?

MRS LOVEIT.
I would die to satisfy that; but I will not, to save you from a thousand racks, do a shameless thing to please your vanity.

DORIMANT.
Farewell, false woman!

MRS LOVEIT.
Do! Go!

DORIMANT.
You will call me back again.

MRS LOVEIT.
Exquisite fiend! I knew you came but to torment me.

Enter Bellinda and Pert

DORIMANT (*surprised*)
Bellinda here!

BELLINDA (*aside*)
He starts and looks pale. The sight of me has touched his guilty soul.

PERT.
'Twas but a qualm, as I said. a little indigestion. The surfeit-water did it, madam, mixed with a little mirabilis.

DORIMANT {*aside*}
I am confounded, and cannot guess how she came hither.

MRS LOVEIT.
'Tis your fortune, Bellinda, ever to be here when I am abused by this prodigy of ill nature.

BELLINDA.
I am amazed to find him here. How has he the face to come near you?

DORIMANT (*aside*)
Here is fine work towards! I never was at such a loss before.

BELLINDA.
One who makes a public profession of breach of faith and ingratitude – I loathe the sight of him.

DORIMANT (*aside*)
There is no remedy. I must submit to their tongues now and some other time bring myself off as well as I can.

BELLINDA.
Other men are wicked, but then they have some sense of shame. He is never well but when he triumphs – nay, glories – to a woman's face in his villainies.

MRS LOVEIT.
You are in the right, Bellinda; but methinks your kindness for me makes you concern yourself too much with him.

BELLINDA.
It does indeed, my dear. His barbarious carriage to you yesterday made me hope you ne'er would see him more, and the very next day to find him here again provokes me strangely. But because I know you love him, I have done.

DORIMANT.
You have reproached me handsomely, and I deserve it for coming hither, but –

PERT.
You must expect it, sir! All woman will hate you for my lady's sake.

DORIMANT {*aside*}
Nay, if she begins too, 'tis time to fly. I shall be scolded to death, else. (*Aside to Bellinda*) I am to blame in some circumstances, I confess; but as to the main, I am not so guilty as you imagine. {*Aloud*} I shall seek a more convenient time to clear myself.

MRS LOVEIT.
Do it now! What impediments are here?

DORIMANT.
I want time, and you want temper.

MRS LOVEIT.
These are weak pretences!

DORIMANT.
You were never more mistaken in your life – and so farewell.

Dorimant flings off

MRS LOVEIT.
Call a footman, Pert. Quickly! I will have him dogged.

PERT.
I wish you would not, for my quiet and your own.

MRS LOVEIT.
I'll find out the infamous causes of all our quarrels, pluck her mask off, and expose her bare-faced to the world!

{Exit Pert}

BELLINDA (*aside*)
Let me but escape this time, I'll never venture more.

MRS LOVEIT.
Bellinda, you shall go with me.

BELLINDA.
I have such a heaviness hangs on me with what I did this morning, I would fain go home and sleep, my dear.

MRS LOVEIT.
Death and eternal darkness! I shall never sleep again. Raging fevers seize the world and make mankind as restless all as I am!

Exit Mrs Loveit

BELLINDA.
I knew him false and helped to make him so. Was not her ruin enough to fright me from the danger? It should have been, but love can take no warning.

Exit Bellinda

Scene Two

Lady Townley's house.

Enter Medley, Young Bellair, Lady Townley, Emilia and {Smirk, a} chaplain.

MEDLEY.
Bear up, Bellair, and do not let us see that repentance in thine we daily do in married faces.

LADY TOWNLEY.
This wedding will strangely surprise my brother when he knows it.

MEDLEY.
Your nephew ought to conceal it for a time, madam. Since marriage has lost its good name, prudent men seldom expose their own reputations till 'tis convenient to justify their wives'.

OLD BELLAIR (*without*)
Where are you all there? Out, adod, will nobody hear?

LADY TOWNLEY.
My brother! Quickly, Mr Smirk, into this closet. You must not be seen yet.

{Smirk} goes into the closet

Enter Old Bellair and Lady Townley's Page

OLD BELLAIR {*to Page*}.
Desire Mr Fourbe to walk into the lower parlour. I will be with him presently.

{Exit Page}

(*To Young Bellair*) Where have you been, sir, you could not wait on me today?

YOUNG BELLAIR.
About a business.

OLD BELLAIR.
Are you so good at business? Adod, I have a business too you shall dispatch out of hand, sir.— Send for a parson, sister. My Lady Woodvill and her daughter are coming.

LADY TOWNLEY.
What need you huddle up things thus?

OLD BELLAIR.
Out a pize! Youth is apt to play the fool, and 'tis not good it should be in their power.

LADY TOWNLEY.
You need not fear your son.

OLD BELLAIR.
He has been idling this morning, and adod, I do not like him. (*To Emilia*) – How dost thou do, sweetheart?

EMILIA.
You are very severe, sir. Married in such haste!

OLD BELLAIR.
Go to, thou'rt a rogue, and I will talk with thee anon. Here's my Lady Woodvill come.

Enter Lady Woodvill, Harriet, and Busy

Welcome, madam. Mr Fourbe's below with the writings.

LADY WOODVILL.
Let us down and make an end, then.

OLD BELLAIR.
Sister, show the way. (*To Young Bellair, who is talking to Harriet*) – Harry, your business lies not there yet! – Excuse him till we have done, lady, and then, adod, he shall be for thee. – Mr Medley, we must trouble you to be a witness.

MEDLEY.
I luckily came for that purpose, sir.

Exeunt Old Bellair, Medley, Young Bellair, Lady Townley and
Lady Woodvill

BUSY {*to Harriet*}.
What will you do, madam?

HARRIET.
Be carried back and mewed up in the country again, run away
here – anything rather than be married to a man I do not care
for. – Dear Emilia, do thou advise me.

EMILIA.
Mr Bellair is engaged, you know.

HARRIET.
I do, but know not what the fear of losing an estate may fright
him to.

EMILIA.
In the desperate condition you are in, you should consult with
some judicious man. What think you of Mr Dorimant?

HARRIET.
I do not think of him at all.

BUSY {*aside*}.
She thinks of nothing else, I am sure.

EMILIA.
How fond your mother was of Mr Courtage.

HARRIET.
Because I contrived the mistake to make a little mirth, you
believe I like the man.

EMILIA.
Mr Bellair believes you love him.

HARRIET.
Men are seldom in the right when they guess at a woman's
mind. Would she whom he loves loved him no better!

BUSY (*aside*)
That's e'en well enough, on all conscience.

EMILIA.
Mr Dorimant has a great deal of wit.

HARRIET.
And takes a great deal of pains to show it.

EMILIA.
He's extremely well-fashioned.

HARRIET.
Affectedly grave, or ridiculously wild and apish.

BUSY.
You defend him still against your mother.

HARRIET.
I would not, were he justly rallied; but I cannot hear anyone
undeservedly railed at.

EMILIA.
Has your woman learnt the song you were so taken with?

HARRIET.
I was fond of a new thing. 'Tis dull at second hearing.

EMILIA.
Mr Dorimant made it.

BUSY.
She knows it, madam, and has made me sing it at least a dozen
times this morning.

HARRIET.
Thy tongue is as impertinent as thy fingers.

EMILIA {*to Busy*}
You have provoked her.

BUSY.
'Tis but singing the song and I shall appease her.

EMILIA.
Prithee, do.

HARRIET.
She has a voice will grate your ears worse than a catcall, and
dresses so ill she's scarce fit to trick up a yeoman's daughter
on a holiday.

Busy sings.

> Song, by Sir C.S.
> As Amoret with Phillis sat
>   One evening on the plain,
> And saw the charming Strephon wait
>   To tell the nymph his pain,
>
> The threat'ning danger to remove,
>   She whispered in her ear,
> 'Ah, Phillis, if you would not love,
>   This shepherd do not hear:
>
> None ever had so strange an art,
>   His passion to convey
> Into a list'ning virgin's heart
>   And steal her soul away.
>
> Fly, fly betimes, for fear you give

Occasion for your fate'.
'In vain', said she, 'in vain I strive.
Alas, 'tis now too late'.

Enter Dorimant

DORIMANT.
'Music so softens and disarms the mind –'

HARRIET.
'That not one arrow does resistance find'.

DORIMANT.
Let us make use of the lucky minute, then.

HARRIET (*aside, turning from Dorimant*)
My love springs with my blood into my face. I dare not look upon him yet.

DORIMANT.
What have we here – the picture of a celebrated beauty giving audience in public to a declared lover?

HARRIET.
Play the dying fop and make the piece complete, sir.

DORIMANT.
What think you if the hint were well improved – the whole mystery of making love pleasantly designed and wrought in a suit of hangings?

HARRIET.
'Twere needless to execute fools in effigy who suffer daily in their own persons.

DORIMANT (*to Emilia, aside*)
Mistress Bride, for such I know this happy day has made you –

EMILIA.
Defer the formal joy you are to give me, and mind your business with her. (*Aloud.*) – Here are dreadful preparations, Mr Dorimant – writings sealing, and a parson sent for.

DORIMANT.
To marry this lady?

BUSY.
Condemned she is; and what will become of her I know not, without you generously engage in a rescue.

DORIMANT.
In this sad condition, madam, I can do no less than offer you my service.

HARRIET.
The obligation is not great; you are the common sanctuary for all young women who run from their relations.

DORIMANT.
I have always my arms open to receive the distressed. But I will open my heart and receive you where none yet did ever enter. You have filled it with a secret, might I but let you know it –

HARRIET.
Do not speak it if you would have me believe it. Your tongue is so famed for falsehood, 'twill do the truth an injury.

Turns away her head

DORIMANT.
Turn not away, then, but look on me and guess it.

HARRIET.
Did you not tell me there was no credit to be given to faces – that women nowadays have their passions as much at will as they have their complexions, and put on joy and sadness, scorn and kindness, with the same ease they do their paint and patches? Are they the only counterfeits?

DORIMANT.
You wrong your own while you suspect my eyes. By all the hope I have in you, the inimitable colour in your cheeks is not more free from art than are the sighs I offer.

HARRIET.
In men who have been long hardened in sin, we have reason to mistrust the first signs of repentance.

DORIMANT.
The prospect of such a heaven will make me persevere and give you marks that are infallible.

HARRIET.
What are those?

DORIMANT.
I will renounce all the joys I have in friendship and wine, sacrifice to you all the interest I have in other women –

HARRIET.
Hold! Though I wish you devout, I would not have you turn fanatic. Could you neglect these a while and make a journey into the country?

DORIMANT.
To be with you, I could live there and never send one thought to London.

HARRIET.

Whate'er you say, I know all beyond Hyde Park's a desert to you, and that no gallantry can draw you farther.

DORIMANT.

That has been the utmost limit of my love; but now my passion knows no bounds, and there's no measure to be taken of what I'll do for you from anything I ever did before.

HARRIET.

When I hear you talk thus in Hampshire, I shall begin to think there may be some little truth enlarged upon.

DORIMANT.

Is this all? Will you not promise me –

HARRIET.

I hate to promise! What we do then is expected from us and wants much of the welcome it finds when it surprises.

DORIMANT.

May I not hope?

HARRIET.

That depends on you and not on me; and 'tis to no purpose to forbid it.

Turns to Busy

BUSY.

Faith, madam, now I perceive the gentleman loves you too. E'en let him know your mind, and torment yourselves no longer.

HARRIET.

Dost think I have no sense of modesty?

BUSY.

Think, if you lose this, you may never have another opportunity.

HARRIET.

May he hate me – a curse that frights me when I speak it! – if ever I do a thing against the rules of decency and honour.

DORIMANT (*to Emilia*)

I am beholding to you for your good intentions, madam.

EMILIA.

I thought the concealing of our marriage from her might have done you better service.

DORIMANT.

Try her again.

EMILIA {*to Harriet*}

What have you resolved, madam? The time draws near.

HARRIET.

To be obstinate and protest against this marriage.

Enter Lady Townley in haste

LADY TOWNLEY (*to Emilia*)

Quickly, quickly, let Mr Smirk out of the closet!

Smirk comes out of the closet.

HARRIET.

A parson! {*To Dorimant*} – Had you laid him in here?

DORIMANT.

I knew nothing of him.

HARRIET.

Should it appear you did, your opinion of my easiness may cost you dear.

Enter Old Bellair, Young Bellair, Medley, and Lady Woodvill

OLD BELLAIR.

Out a pize, the canonical hour is almost past! Sister, is the man of God come?

LADY TOWNLEY {*indicating Smirk*}

He waits your leisure.

OLD BELLAIR {*to Smirk*}

By your favour, sir – Adod, a pretty spruce fellow! What may we call him?

LADY TOWNLEY.

Mr Smirk – my Lady Biggot's chaplain.

OLD BELLAIR.

A wise woman, adod she is! The man will serve for the flesh as well as the spirit. – Please you, sir, to commission a young couple to go to bed together a God's name? – Harry!

YOUNG BELLAIR.

Here, sir.

OLD BELLAIR.

Out a pize! Without your mistress in your hand?

SMIRK.

Is this the gentleman?

OLD BELLAIR.

Yes, sir.

SMIRK.
Are you not mistaken, sir?

OLD BELLAIR.
Adod, I think not, sir!

SMIRK.
Sure you are, sir.

OLD BELLAIR.
You look as if you would forbid the banns, Mr Smirk. I hope you have no pretension to the lady!

SMIRK.
Wish him joy, sir! I have done him the good office today already.

OLD BELLAIR.
Out a pize! What do I hear?

LADY TOWNLEY.
Never storm, brother. The truth is out.

OLD BELLAIR.
How say you, sir? Is this your wedding day?

YOUNG BELLAIR.
It is, sir

OLD BELLAIR.
And, adod, it shall be mine too. (*To Emilia*) Give me thy hand, sweetheart. {*She refuses*} What dost thou mean? Give me thy hand, I say!

Emilia kneels and Young Bellair

LADY TOWNLEY.
Come, come, give her your blessing. This is the woman your son loved and is married to.

OLD BELLAIR.
Ha! Cheated! Cozened! And by your contrivance, sister!

LADY TOWNLEY.
What would you do with her? She's a rogue, and you can't abide her.

MEDLEY.
Shall I hit her a pat for you, sir?

OLD BELLAIR.
Adod, you are all rogues, and I never will forgive you.

{*Flings away, as if to exit*}

LADY TOWNLEY.
Whither? Whither away?

MEDLEY.
Let him go and cool awhile.

LADY WOODVILL (*to Dorimant*)
Here's a business broke out now, Mr Courtage. I am made a fine fool of.

DORIMANT.
You see the old gentleman knew nothing of it.

LADY WOODVILL.
I find he did not. I shall have some trick put upon me, if I stay in this wicked town any longer. – Harriet, dear child, where art thou? I'll into the country straight.

OLD BELLAIR.
Adod, madam, you shall hear me first –

Enter Mrs Loveit and Bellinda

MRS LOVEIT.
Hither my man dogged him.

BELLINDA.
Yonder he stands, my dear.

MRS LOVEIT.
I see him, (*aside*) and with him the face that has undone me. Oh, that I were but where I might throw out the anguish of my heart! Here it must rage within and break it.

LADY TOWNLEY.
Mrs Loveit! Are you afraid to come forward?

MRS LOVEIT.
I was amazed to see so much company here in a morning. The occasion sure is extraordinary.

DORIMANT (*aside*)
Loveit and Bellinda! The devil owes me a shame today, and I think never will have done paying it.

MRS LOVEIT.
Married! Dear Emilia, how am I transported with the news!

HARRIET (*to Dorimant*)
I little thought Emilia was the woman Mr Bellair was in love with. I'll chide her for not trusting me with the secret.

DORIMANT.
How do you like Mrs Loveit?

HARRIET.
She's a famed mistress of yours, I hear.

DORIMANT.
She has been, on occasion.

OLD BELLAIR (*to Lady Woodvill*)
Adod, madam, I cannot help it.

LADY WOODVILL.
You need make no more apologies, sir.

EMILIA (*to Mrs Loveit*)
The old gentleman's excusing himself to my Lady
Woodvill.

MRS LOVEIT.
Ha, ha, ha! I never heard of anything so pleasant.

HARRIET (*to Dorimant*)
She's extremely overjoyed at something.

DORIMANT.
At nothing. She is one of those hoiting ladies who gaily fling
themselves about and force a laugh when their aching hearts
are full of discontent and malice.

MRS LOVEIT.
Oh heaven! I was never so near killing myself with laughing. –
Mr Dorimant, are you a brideman?

LADY WOODVILL.
Mr Dorimant! Is this Mr Dorimant, madam?

MRS LOVEIT.
If you doubt it, your daughter can resolve you, I suppose.

LADY WOODVILL.
I am cheated too, basely cheated!

OLD BELLAIR.
Out a pize, what's here? More knavery yet?

LADY WOODVILL.
Harriet! On my blessing, come away, I charge you.

HARRIET.
Dear mother, do but stay and hear me.

LADY WOODVILL.
I am betrayed, and thou art undone, I fear.

HARRIET.
Do not fear it. I have not, nor never will, do anything against
my duty. Believe me, dear mother, do!

DORIMANT (*to Mrs Loveit*)
I had trusted you with this secret but that I knew the violence
of your nature would ruin my fortune – as now unluckily it

has. I thank you, madam.

MRS LOVEIT.
She's an heiress, I know, and very rich.

DORIMANT.
To satisfy you, I must give up my interest wholly to my love.
Had you been a reasonable woman, I might have secured 'em
both and been happy.

MRS LOVEIT.
You might have trusted me with anything of this kind, you
know you might. Why did you go under a wrong name?

DORIMANT.
The story is too long to tell you know. Be satisfied; this is the
business, this is the mask that has kept me from you.

BELLINDA (*aside*)
He's tender of my honour, though he's cruel to my love.

MRS LOVEIT.
Was it no idle mistress, then?

DORIMANT.
Believe me – a wife, to repair the ruins of my estate that needs
it.

MRS LOVEIT.
The knowledge of this makes my grief hang lighter on my
soul, but I shall never more be happy.

DORIMANT.
Bellinda –

BELLINDA.
Do not think of clearing yourself with me. It is impossible.
Do all men break their words thus?

DORIMANT.
Th' extravagant words they speak in love. 'Tis as
unreasonable to expect we should perform all we promise
then, as do all we threaten when we are angry. When I see you
next –

BELLINDA.
Take no notice of me, and I shall not hate you.

DORIMANT.
How came you to Mrs Loveit?

BELLINDA.
By a mistake the chairmen made for went of my giving them
directions.

DORIMANT.
'Twas a pleasant one. We must meet again.

BELLINDA.
Never.

DORIMANT.
Never?

BELLINDA.
When we do, may I be as infamous as you are false.

LADY TOWNLEY.
Men of Mr Dorimant's character always suffer in the general opinion of the world.

MEDLEY.
You can make no judgment of a witty man from common fame, considering the prevailing faction, madam.

OLD BELLAIR.
Adod, he's in the right.

MEDLEY.
Besides, 'tis a common error among women to believe too well of them they know and too ill of them they don't.

OLD BELLAIR.
Adod, he observes well.

LADY TOWNLEY.
Believe me, madam, you will find Mr Dorimant as civil a gentleman as you thought Mr Courtage.

HARRIET.
If you would but know him better –

LADY WOODVILL.
You have a mind to know him better? Come away! You shall never see him more.

HARRIET.
Dear mother, stay!

LADY WOODVILL.
I won't be consenting to your ruin.

HARRIET.
Were my fortune in your power –

LADY WOODVILL.
Your person is.

HARRIET.
Could I be disobedient, I might take it out of yours and put it into his.

LADY WOODVILL.
'Tis that you would be at! You would marry this Dorimant!

HARRIET.
I cannot deny it. I would, and never will marry any other man.

LADY WOODVILL.
Is this the duty that you promised?

HARRIET.
But I will never marry him against your will.

LADY WOODVILL (aside)
She knows the way to melt my heart. (To Harriet) – Upon yourself light your undoing.

MEDLEY (to Old Bellair)
Come, sir, you have not the heart any longer to refuse your blessing.

OLD BELLAIR.
Adod, I ha' not. – Rise, and God bless you both! Make much of her, Harry; she deserves thy kindness. (To Emilia.) Adod, sirrah, I did not think it had been in thee.

Enter Sir Fopling and his Page

SIR FOPLING.
'Tis a damned windy day. Hey, page! Is my periwig right?

PAGE.
A little out of order, sir.

SIR FOPLING.
Pox o' this apartment! It wants an antechamber to adjust one's self in. (To Mrs Loveit.) – Madam, I came from your house, and your servants directed me hither.

MRS LOVEIT.
I will give order hereafter they shall direct you better.

SIR FOPLING.
The great satisfaction I had in the Mall last night has given me much disquiet since.

MRS LOVEIT.
'Tis likely to give me more than I desire.

SIR FOPLING {aside}
What the devil makes her so reserved? – Am I guilty of an indiscretion, madam?

MRS LOVEIT.
You will be of a great one, if you continue your mistake, sir.

SIR FOPLING.
Something puts you out of humour.

MRS LOVEIT.
The most foolish, inconsiderable thing that ever did.

SIR FOPLING.
Is it in my power?

MRS LOVEIT.
To hang or drown it. Do one of 'em, and trouble me no more.

SIR FOPLING.
So *fière? Serviteur*, madam! – Medley, where's Dorimant?

MEDLEY.
Methinks the lady has not made you those advances today she did last night, Sir Fopling.

SIR FOPLING.
Prithee, do not talk of her.

MEDLEY.
She would be a *bonne fortune*.

SIR FOPLING.
Not to me at present.

MEDLEY.
How so?

SIR FOPLING.
An intrigue now would be but a temptation to me to throw away that vigour on one which I mean shall shortly make my court to the whole sex in a ballet.

MEDLEY.
Wisely considered, Sir Fopling.

SIR FOPLING.
No one woman is worth the loss of a cut in a caper.

MEDLEY.
Not when 'tis so universally designed.

LADY WOODVILL.
Mr Dorimant, everyone has spoke so much in your behalf that I can no longer doubt but I was in the wrong.

MRS LOVEIT {*to Bellinda*}
There's nothing but falsehood and impertinence in this world. All men are villains or fools. Take example from my misfortunes. Bellinda, if thou wouldst be happy, give thyself wholly up to goodness.

HARRIET {*to Mrs Loveit*}
Mr Dorimant has been your God Almighty long enough. 'Tis time to think of another.

MRS LOVEIT {*to Bellinda*}
Jeered by her! I will lock myself up in my house and never see the world again.

HARRIET.
A nunnery is the more fashionable place for such a retreat and has been the fatal consequence of many a *belle passion*.

MRS LOVEIT (*aside*).
Hold, heart, till I get home! Should I answer, 'twould make her triumph greater.

Is going out

DORIMANT.
Your hand, Sir Fopling –

SIR FOPLING.
Shall I wait upon you, madam?

MRS LOVEIT.
Legion of fools, as many devils take thee!

Exit Mrs Loveit.

MEDLEY.
Dorimant! I pronounce thy reputation clear, and henceforward, when I would know anything of woman, I will consult no other oracle.

SIR FOPLING.
Stark mad, by all that's handsome! – Dorimant, thou hast engaged me in a pretty business.

DORIMANT.
I have not leisure now to talk about it.

OLD BELLAIR.
Out a pize, what does this man of mode do here again?

LADY TOWNLEY.
He'll be an excellent entertainment within, brother, and is luckily come to raise the mirth of the company.

LADY WOODVILL.
Madam, I take my leave of you.

LADY TOWNLEY.
What do you mean, madam?

LADY WOODVILL.
To go this afternoon part of my way to Hartley –

OLD BELLAIR.

Adod, you shall stay and dine first! Come, we will all be good friends, and you shall give Mr Dorimant leave to wait upon you and your daughter in the country.

LADY WOODVILL.

If his occasions bring him that way, I have now so good an opinion of him, he shall be welcome.

HARRIET.

To a great, rambling, lone house that looks as it were not inhabited, the family's so small. There you'll find my mother, an old lame aunt, and myself, sir, perched up on chairs at a distance in a large parlour, sitting moping like three or four melancholy birds in a spacious volary. Does not this stagger your resolution?

DORIMANT.

Not at all, madam. The first time I saw you, you left me with the pangs of love upon me, and this day my soul has quite given up her liberty.

HARRIET.

This is more dismal than the country. – Emilia, pity me who am going to that sad place. Methinks I hear the hateful noise of rooks already – kaw, kaw, kaw. There's music in the worst cry in London – 'My dill and cucumbers to pickle'.

OLD BELLAIR.

Sister, knowing of this matter, I hope you have provided us some good cheer.

LADY TOWNLEY.

I have, brother, and the fiddles too.

OLD BELLAIR.

Let 'em strike up then. The young lady shall have a dance before she departs.

Dance

(*After the dance*) So now we'll in, and make this an arrant wedding day.

(*To the pit*)

And if these honest gentlemen rejoice,
Adod, the boy has made a happy choice.

Exeunt omnes

THE EPILOGUE

BY MR DRYDEN

Most modern wits such monstrous fools have shown,
They seemed not of heav'n's making, but their own.
Those nauseous harlequins in farce may pass,
But there goes more to a substantial ass!
Something of man must be exposed to view,
That, gallants, it may more resemble you.
Sir Fopling is a fool so nicely writ,
The ladies would mistake him for a wit,
And when he sings, talks loud, and cocks, would cry:
'I vow, methinks, he's pretty company –
So brisk, so gay, so travelled, so refined!'
As he took pains to graft upon his kind,
True fops help nature's work, and go to school
To file and finish God A'mighty's fool.
Yet none Sir Fopling him, or him, can call –
He's knight o' the shire and represents ye all.
From each he meets, he culls whate'er he can:
Legion's his name, a people in a man.
His bulky folly gathers as it goes,
And, rolling o'er you, like a snowball grows.
His various modes from various fathers follow;
One taught the toss, and one the new French wallow.
His sword-knot, this, his cravat, this designed –
And this, the yard-long snake he twirls behind.
From one, the sacred periwig he gained,
Which wind ne'er blew, nor touch of hat profaned;
Another's diving bow he did adore,
Which with a shog casts all the hair before,
Till he with full decorum brings it back
And rises with a water spaniel shake.
As for his songs (the ladies' dear delight),
Those sure he took from most of you who write.
Yet every man is safe from what he feared,
For no one fool is hunted from the herd.